Life and the Student

Life and the Student

Roadside Notes on Human Nature, Society, and Letters

Charles Horton Cooley
With a new introduction by Jonathan B. Imber

Transaction Publishers
New Brunswick (U.S.A.) and London (U.K.)

This book is printed on acid-free paper that meets the American National Standard for Permanence of Paper for Printed Library Materials.

Library of Congress Catalog Number: 2014032413
ISBN: 978-1-4128-5478-8
Printed in the United States of America

Library of Congress Cataloging-in-Publication Data

Cooley, Charles Horton, 1864-1929.
Life and the student : roadside notes on human nature, society, and letters / by Charles Horton Cooley.
pages cm
Originally published: New York : A.A. Knopft, 1927.
Includes bibliographical references and index.
ISBN 978-1-4128-5478-8
1. Life. I. Title.
BD431.C68 2014
128--dc23

2014032413

Contents

Introduction

The Vocation of Charles Horton Cooley

Jonathan B. Imber

Writing in 2014 about life and the student, I am struck by how little of what Charles Horton Cooley addressed has changed since the publication of his book in 1927. Eighty-seven years is a long time to be suspended in the publishing purgatory known as "out of print." But there is an impending redemption for all books rediscovered and reread with the benefit of hindsight and the clarity (and challenges) of present circumstances. This book, subtitled *Roadside Notes on Human Nature, Society, and Letters,* is the last one that Cooley would publish before he died on May 8, 1929 at the age of sixty-five. By reintroducing the observations and aphorisms contained in this collection, I aim to say more about life and the student in particular. Cooley's thoughts and observations range farther and wider than that particular subject, but the anchor of his thoughtful convictions is best understood by the primary importance he gave to teaching and to its implications for life, liberty, and the pursuit of happiness.

Cooley's motivation for publishing these reflections is recounted by one of his colleagues at the University of Michigan, Arthur Evans Wood, following Cooley's death:

> The life-history of this book he gave to us at a meeting of our Sociology Club. He had previously told me that he was working on something which he hoped might be of value to students in their intellectual life. It seems that for years he had been making random notes on his reading and reflections. When, at last, he thought of publication he went over his notes, concluded that they were unsatisfactory, abandoned them, and made a fresh start. When, again, the matter of publication was considered, he sent

> the manuscript to his old publisher [likely Scribner's] with the result that it was rejected. Cooley said, amusingly, "I suppose some editor of educational texts got hold of the thing and concluded that I had gone crazy." Happily, the volume came to light through another source. [Alfred A. Knopf] In it one discovers the real Cooley better than through any of his other books.[1]

Another remark by Wood in his appreciation of Cooley's defense of the principle of democracy is worth bearing in mind going forward:

> Since the war, in view of the defeat of the principle in various governments in Europe, and because of attacks upon it by some of our shallower journalists, I sometimes have wondered why Cooley did not come to a fresh defense of his principles. On second thought, however, it was clear that he had no mind for contending against men of straw. Sufficient for him was it that the principle had been stated in his writings. Its fortunes in the world of affairs were not his primary concern.[2]

Cooley has been described as a herald of small-town America, the kind of place called a "community." Everett Cherrington Hughes said somewhere that community extends as far as a man is talked about. In Cooley's case, he was a fixture, as was his father before him, at the University of Michigan at Ann Arbor. But *Life and the Student* reveals that his observations as a sociologist were not confined to that single place (nor to a single species: his most famous formulation of the "looking-glass self" is reprised here with the observation that "A dog differs from a cat in having a looking-glass self [37]). He noted "the vitality, force, and promise . . . from the crowd of foreigners at Revere Beach near Boston" (25). A century later some things have not changed except for who visits that beach and where they have come from beyond American shores.

---

[1] Arthur Evans Wood, "Charles Horton Cooley: An Appreciation," *American Journal of Sociology* 35, no. 5 (March 1930), 708. Cooley had several years earlier praised the appointment of Wood who developed courses and research on social work. See Charles Horton Cooley, "The Development of Sociology at Michigan," in *Sociological Theory and Social Research: Being Selected Papers of Charles Horton Cooley*, ed. Robert Cooley Angell (New York: Henry Holt, 1930) 3–14.

[2] Ibid., 714. For other reviews of this book at the time of its publication, see Read Bain, "A Sociologist Looks at Life," *Social Forces* 6, no. 3 (March 1928) 479–80; G. T. Buswell, "Review," *The Elementary School Journal* 28, no. 8 (April 1928) 635; H. L. Lurie, "Review," *Social Service Review* 1, no. 4 (December 1927) 669–70; Arthur J. Todd, "Review," *American Journal of Sociology* 33, no. 6 (May 1928) 1006–10.

Automobiles and Freedom

Cooley knew the enduring predicaments of a nation that displayed the public tensions of old and new, small and large, familiar and different. He opens *Life and the Student* with reflections on the automobile, which by the 1920s certainly was a familiar but still new and growing ingredient of social interactions. The sociologist, Orlando Patterson, has written on freedom and the transformational nature of America's romance with the automobile and the open road.[3] Cooley anticipates that connection when he writes, "I like this traveling by your own will and means, trusting to your own skill, liable to adventures" (1). The theme of trust is embedded in his several remarks on how "completely you are dependent for safety on the man in the passing car!" (1). And the corollaries to the mere existence of cars abound, inspiring him to comment that "this childlike preoccupation of our people with mechanism is not such a bad thing; it keeps them innocently busy at least. Tinkering is a national pastime . . ." (2). In addition, and more important, there are implications for democratic order: "All of our modern means of communication facilitate democracy by multiplying contacts. The automobile does this in rather a peculiar way, by causing all classes actually to rub against one another, as it were, on the open road. It brings many sorts of people face-to-face, and mostly under fellowship conditions" (2).

Freedom encourages more than the exercising of "your own will." It fosters greater familiarity with many kinds of differences in all aspects of social life.[4] Yet Cooley writes, "Any notion of freedom that does not include continuity is illusive. We are free only as there is opened to us

---

[3] Orlando Patterson, "The American View of Freedom: What We Say, What We Mean," *Society* 38, no. 4 (May/June 2001) 37–45. Between 1900 and 1930, the estimated number of automobiles on American roads grew from 14,000 to over 20 million. See http://web.bryant.edu/~ehu/h364/materials/cars/index.htm. See also Hans-Joachim Schubert's brief account of Cooley's work for the Interstate Commerce Commission on the transportation system in Charles Horton Cooley, *On Self and Social Organization*, edited and with an introduction by Hans-Joachim Schubert (Chicago: University of Chicago Press, 1998) 7–9.

[4] In *Social Organization*, first published in 1909, Cooley makes no mention of the automobile, but he gives ample attention to new social connections made by access to the newspaper: "What a strange practice it is, when you think of it, that a man should sit down to his breakfast table and, instead of conversing with his wife, and children, hold before his face a sort of screen on which is inscribed a world-wide gossip." Charles Horton Cooley, *Social Organization: A Study of the Larger Mind* (New York: Charles Scribner's, 1909), 83. That "sort of screen" matters with regard to the social connections it forms and deforms, and not whether it is a newspaper or an IPad.

an orderly process of growth from what we are to something better" (4). Before the anonymity of interstate highways and the increased frequency of road rage and other perilous distractions to driving, such as alcohol or texting, Cooley's vision of the automobile's contribution to human freedom was largely uncontestable. But this vision was not necessarily consistent with reality. He readily acknowledged the social forces that also led to pessimism about America's future: "The family has lost it permanent home and much of its inner solidarity; economic function is transitory; the church is questioned and neglected, our country is too far away for common uses. We splice the broken strands with such makeshifts as we find and trust that will knit them up" (4). Cooley recognized the changing conditions of stability, which produced in group life and the social imagination new and sometimes disturbing encounters with the ways that old connections were being fractured. In alluding to, without naming, such figures as Rockefeller and Carnegie, he remarks that the basis for recognition of individual achievement prompts more and more people to "seek to associate their names and achievements with lasting institutions."[5]

The ambition to be known, revered, and remembered has a great deal to do with the meanings of wealth beyond its acquisition. Cooley's evolutionism tended toward promoting moderation and the middle ground, both of which, it turns out, are the most difficult positions to maintain in the face of what he ably describes as the similar perspectives of radicals and reactionaries: "Radicals and reactionaries are in alliance; each profits by the other; they mutually confer importance. Militarism and pacifism, Tolstoi and Bernhardi, go arm in arm; capitalism incites lawlessness in order to make its own rule appear necessary; the ascetic and the libertine are kindred spirits. These extremes are the common antagonist of moderate people who wish freedom and order" (7). A remarkable sensibility emerges in Cooley's sociological disposition. He saw through the ambitions of those who pull back and those who push forward too hard: "Nothing more sheep-like than a flock of young rebels" (7). This last admonition has less to do with the bravado of youth than with the seductions of ideology.[6]

[5] This melding of individuals with institutions (especially in the case of higher education) has devolved into a welter of names attached to nearly everything that stands still in public and private spheres. See Jonathan B. Imber, "Generosity, Vulnerability, and Immortality," in *Conversations on Philanthropy*, vol. 6, "Identity, Interests, and Philanthropic Commerce," (Alexandria, VA: DonorsTrust, 2009), 15–20.

[6] See Jonathan B. Imber, "Values, Politics, and Science: The Influence of Social Movements on Sociology—Other-Directed Rebels," in *Contemporary Sociology* 28, no. 3 (May 1999), 255–59. See also Christian Smith, *The Sacred Project of American Sociology* (New York: Oxford University Press, 2014).

The Radical and Reactionary

Charles Horton Cooley, for all the laurels he earned as a sociologist and sociological theorist, was first and foremost a teacher.[7] This book, interspersed with his reflections on the art and artifice of that vocation, speaks to a wisdom that occasionally has been well expressed by more recent and similarly situated teachers in colleges and universities.[8] In some ways distinct from Max Weber's call for a disinterested social science, Cooley shifted the emphasis from the production of research (Weber's approach) to the obligations of teaching: "A teacher finds that extreme views do not survive comparative study. How many fanatical radicals and reactionaries have I seen thawed, as it were, by hearing lectures as by finding, in discussion, what fellows of their own sort have to say on the other side" (8). The rise of what Cooley terms "fanatical radicals and reactionaries" anticipates a half century later the broad politicization of higher education.[9] Weber and Cooley were reacting in their

[7] My assertion goes against obvious and prevailing debates that seek to establish the visibility and rank of sociological theorists in a canon. And these debates are not at all irrelevant to understanding Cooley. See Glenn Jacobs, "Influence and Canonical Supremacy: An Analysis of How George Herbert Mead Demoted Charles Horton Cooley in the Sociological Canon." *Journal of the History of the Behavioral Sciences* 45, no. 2 (Spring 2009): 117–144; and Glenn Jacobs, *Charles Horton Cooley: Imagining Social Reality* (Amherst, MA: University of Massachusetts Press, 2006). See also Roscoe C. Hinkle, "Charles Horton Cooley's General Sociological Orientation." *Sociological Inquiry* 8, no. 1 (Winter 1967): 5–20. I am arguing for Cooley another status that pertains to the nature of his vocation, a term that has no scientific measure. Its external validation, unlike a scientific fact, belongs to another realm equally important to social life. Vocation is a spiritual idea, observable in others but with no handbook of procedures or absolutely required evidence to confirm its existence. As Cooley concluded, "And virtue, the most important distinction of all, is independent alike of wealth, calling and culture. The real upper class, that which is doing the most for the onward movement of human life, is not to be discerned by any visible sign. The more inward or spiritual a trait is, the less it is dependent upon what are ordinarily understood as class distinctions." *Social Organization*, 250.

[8] See Jay Parini, The Art of Teaching (New York: Oxford University Press, 2005). Parini has little to say (and rightly so) about the shape and form of institutions or the significance of his art for "higher education." This contrasts to the enormous number of books devoted, in Cooley's sense, to the reform of everything, whether in the form of a hopeful nostalgia or a critique of students' materialism spurred on by their meritocratic ambitions. One illustration of the temptation to abandon vocation for administration, though not completely, is Andrew Delbanco, College: What it Was, Is, and Should Be (Princeton, NJ: Princeton University Press, 2012).

[9] Elsewhere in this volume, Cooley elaborates on the unique characteristics of the sociological perspective, describing in terms reminiscent of Wilhelm Dilthey's distinction between the *Naturwisssenschaften* and the *Geisteswissenschaften*, how "Social investigation calls for a habit of mind unlike that of spatial science, and it is rare that men trained in the latter do sound work in it. Their precise and circumscribed sense of fact tends to incapacitate them for that sympathetic grasp of complex human conditions which is the prime need in social studies" (151).

time to social movements that had yet to insinuate themselves substantially into higher education. With the post–Second World War democratization of higher education in Europe and America, suspicion and protest replaced discussion, and the goals of research became allied with the ambitions of social movements. Perhaps in this respect both Weber and Cooley were naïve to hope for an insulation from politics that would not inevitably also be viewed as insular. Yet Cooley maintained his focus on the goal of teaching, never denying or avoiding the inevitability of political, social, and economic realities but also standing against the easy conflation of conviction with knowledge. This conflation is not a philosophical puzzle on the order of debates about the fact/value distinction. The stakes are about temperament and the attitude of the teacher. For Cooley, teaching as a vocation required a willingness to acknowledge the authenticity of conflicting values and to do so in ways that affected his students' capacity to embrace a fuller appreciation that such conflict is an inevitable and productive feature of democratic order.

In another illustration of Cooley's feeling intellect, he anticipated the perils of meritocracy long before it was given its now conventional name. Referring to "an aristocracy of brains," he questions the call for it to be the exclusive provider of social guidance: "That we need to be more guided by intelligence, wherever found, is most true; but if you mean that we are to look for this in a class, you are all wrong. A sound social intelligence is a function of the whole community . . . We must improve as a whole" (12). Cooley may have understood that in the absence of a hereditary aristocracy, America risked using its brains or its wealth in antidemocratic and overly self-interested ways, which is to say, in ways that forfeit responsibility to the "whole community."[10] That kind of responsibility was diminished substantially when the draft was abolished in favor of an all-volunteer military in the 1970s, coinciding with the rise of a cognitive elite (and its disproportionate representation in the university) beyond its predecessor, the managerial

[10] Contemporary arguments about growing inequality may differ in what counts as inequality, with more emphasis put on material conditions from the left and more emphasis put on cognitive differences from the right. Such exclusive emphases may conceal the essential relationship between the two. See Jonathan B. Imber, "The Far Side of Meritocracy." *The American Interest* 8, no. 2 (November/December 2012): 91–96.

elite. While sociologists in the generation after Cooley were writing about "organization man" and "the lonely crowd," a powerful reshaping of opportunity was also taking place, promoting new criteria of conformity for admission to higher education. It would take another half century for the aristocracy of brains, which he identified as already problematic, to reveal its lasting impact on American life.

Already in 1927, Cooley recognized the enduring nature of the color line, a discussion of which follows directly from his conviction about "how poor American life would be without immigrants . . ." (12). The concept of "race" combined outwardly observed features with religion and nationality, thus giving priority to each social group's claims for both acceptance and rejection of and by other groups. Objecting to the then popular debates about racial superiority and inferiority, he defended the rights of groups to retain their identities but asked, "Why not cherish the individuality of races, as we do that of persons, without raising the vague and invidious question of superiority?" (14).[11] He understood the social psychology of race friction: "Contempt of another race is often one of those methods by which people suffering from a sense of inferiority seek to stimulate their self-respect. A white man, feeling that he is looked down upon by other white men, takes it out on the Negro. Where one race has formerly been enslaved by the other this attitude will be peculiarly lasting and arrogant" (14). The prescience of these observations was in keeping with his opposition to restrictions on opportunity for any group, but he acknowledged the most salient truth about the "primary group" and its central role in establishing (and maintaining) the priorities of living: "We talk equal opportunity, but which of us is not striving to make it even more unequal than it is by getting privileges for his children? Moreover the privileged class strives as a body (though unconsciously) to increase its privileges. Yet we are sincere, perhaps, in wishing that things might, in general, be more equal, and, unless our own advantages are at stake, are not unwilling to do something toward this end" (20).

[11] See Charles Horton Cooley, "Genius, Fame and the Comparison of Races." in *Sociological Theory and Social Research: Being Selected Papers of Charles Horton Cooley*, ed. Robert Cooley Angell (New York: Henry Holt, 1930) 121–59. See also Leon R. Kass, "Intelligence and the Social Scientist." *The Public Interest*, no. 120, Summer 1995, 64–78.

What Cooley described as an unconscious process, that is, what parents do for their children as a matter of course, does not obviously relieve people of another sentiment that embraces, perhaps more out of guilt than anything else, the inherent unfairness of life. His sociology was a balancing act between these unconscious sentiments that also produce in their extreme forms both radicals and reactionaries. There is thus much to commend in Cooley's remarks about the nature of privilege and about its implications for understanding class divisions and class consciousness. He explicitly uses the term "class consciousness" in much the way that Marx and his successors used it, and he rejects explanations using "vague theories of 'the survival of the fittest'" to account for "crime, vice, and misery" the responsibility for which "goes with power" and the blame for which belongs to "the educated and well-to-do classes" (21). This is Cooley's adaptation and rendition of *noblesse oblige*.[12] The American upper class is in his estimation a unique formation, a creature of democracy, exhibiting counter-tendencies between a wish to be separate from the public in living and lifestyle but a desire to "seek general publicity in the newspapers" (22). Without naming it as we do today, celebrity culture with its fundamental motivation to be known by others, is an artifact of democracy and the emerging and powerful alliance that celebrity seeking has with therapeutic culture. Cooley concluded that publicity seeking was a sign of an absence of caste sentiment, but the control of personality that caste historically demanded would in years subsequent to his conclusion become the basis for the condemnation of narcissism that has yet to be fully given its historical due.[13]

Literature and Education

Cooley's reflections on literature are recapitulations of his attitude toward social life more generally. His erudition is less important than his various statements on the function of erudition, offering a different perspective on the purpose of "name-dropping." He writes, "I read the French moralists—de la Rochefoucauld, La Bruyère,

[12] Cooley also explicitly refers to *noblesse oblige* with respect to students' higher ambitions: "American students have some of the virtues of aristocracy—magnanimity, courage, self-respect, group discipline, fair play (among themselves), sometimes engaging manners. Possibly they may yet proceed to *noblesse oblige* and the finer kinds of ambition" (180).

[13] See Elizabeth Lunbeck, *The Americanization of Narcissism* (Cambridge, MA: Harvard University Press, 2014).

Pascal—not so much for the value of their ideas, however great that may be, as because I like the company of men who are interested in such ideas" (30). He remarks on what makes a book satisfying; what gives a sentence its special character; and how writing and the thoughts behind it can be held hostage to the expectations of others. Writers as diverse as Gibbon, Macaulay, Thoreau, Spencer, Emerson, Nietzsche, Whitman, Bergson, Frost, James, Dewey, Johnson, Pater, Dante, Shakespeare, and many others are mentioned not simply in passing but as illustrations of different varieties of success and failure in the ambitions of literature. In much of what he says about these ambitions, Cooley is defining the conditions for the inevitability of literary canons: "In general . . . a failure to see merit in long-accepted authors throws more light on the critic than on the authors. There are substantial grounds for these reputations—one school of critics may be fooled, but not several, from different times and cultures—and if a man does not feel them it means either that his mind is limited or that he has not taken the trouble to bring it into real contact" (43). The "canon" is a social species of ideas, organized less by subject than by what it teaches over and over again. Observing the repetition of experience as it is heightened by literary insight was Cooley's essential methodology. Such a method does not preclude numbers and counting, but it gives priority to the canonical lessons of life even as that life is buffeted and transformed by forces greater than any one person or group. The expectations of an audience were least important to him: "I work most effectively for a vague and remote public. Immediate publicity, or the prospect of it, is an unneeded and disquieting stimulant" (46). And he insisted that "Originality begins in our reaction to the necessary events of life, to things that come up hard against us" (56).

To be an educated person in Cooley's vision was to emulate what Josef Pieper described in his short book, *Leisure: The Basis of Culture*. This vision pertained to the writer's vocation.[14] He was dead set against magazines: "The smaller the bits in which one publishes the more he exposes himself to be dissolved in the surrounding medium. In a larger whole he is more likely to preserve his real self" (47). The book, then,

[14] Cooley also commended this vision as the basis for the incipient vocation of the student: "I should advise a boy who is ambitious for culture to go to college, if he can, for the sake of leisure, books and possibly-inspiring persons" (179).

was favored because of the fullness of self poured into, and preserved by, it. Ego "dissolved in the surrounding medium" is by far the more common fate for the expression of ideas today by those whose ambition is to be heard and known. The flashes of acknowledgment that may come with being known repeatedly, were hardly bright enough to impress Cooley's sensibility about what might better assure canonical status. To write less and to take longer were acts that invoked the long view about such matters, a risk that the most ambitious and often brightest are not willing to consider. Ambition itself was not the culprit: "The ambition to appear sophisticated, or what amounts to the same, the fear of appearing naïve, is a fence to keep us within the commonplace" (57). This ironic formulation suggests more than an antipathy toward many of the ambitions of academic life, where sophistication is expressed in jargon and a kind of contrariness toward the things that are obviously true. The "commonplace" is presently defined by over-sophistication about so many things Cooley took for granted. His defense of naiveté is a deference to personal, group, and national strengths that are now held out as indications and expressions of arrogant power.

In this way, Cooley's account of sociology, art, and science, to which he devotes a section of this book, reveals others' underlying animus toward what began in his lifetime as a new enterprise in search of its role as an academic and scholarly subject: "Since the facts of sociology are those of personality and human change, and since these are precisely what the men of other sciences are taught to eliminate, it would be strange if they did not regard this science with distrust" (79). And, "We hear it questioned whether sociology is a science or a philosophy. It is both, and an art also" (79). Cooley anticipated here the importance of ethnography to the stock of knowledge that going forward would be called sociological. His persistence in distinguishing sociology from other endeavors may reflect a defensiveness about the discipline, but what he knew already in 1927 was that sociology and sociologists were not synonymous with each other. He knew without saying so explicitly that the many factors which determined the status of a discipline would involve debates about boundaries and accepted knowledge, all of which would determine support for and resistance to the work of those claiming to represent it. This status grew out of the attraction of new generations to the possibilities of new insight into enduring problems and forces in society. At the same time, sociologists would argue among themselves about the nature of their discipline, some upholding Cooley's sympathetic understanding and others embracing abstraction and quantification.[15]

The Vocation of the Teacher

Cooley was a deeply educated man, someone for whom the wide range of great literary figures was an invitation to, and promise of, connection to that greater whole which is humanity. But his humanism was neither scholastic nor did it seek to advance ideas exclusively of one writer or another. Instead he read and wrote in order to be, in my estimation, an example to students and colleagues who would then be free to decide how to understand themselves and others more fully. This is one way to consider two comments he made about controversy: "Let our struggle be with facts, with life, rather with other writers. We cannot have the spirit of truth and the spirit of controversy at the same time." And "One who writes controversy digs his own grave. Only serene thoughts will last" (61). A teacher's serenity requires protection from controversy so as to measure and evaluate it in the flow of events and the reality of circumstances that incite emotion and thus threaten to challenge that serenity. Cooley knew well that there would always be controversy and those willing and needing to engage it. That so many teachers today find themselves engaged in, rather than removed from, controversy speaks to failures of individual and institutional will. Academic freedom is conflated with the First Amendment, creating opportunities for incitement and mean-spiritedness that work to replace teaching with new forms of preaching.

His account of being a college teacher leads Cooley to remark on many aspects of his vocation that do not routinely receive much attention. The teacher, he says, "is a dramatist, who must conceive his subject freshly for each performance, and he will hardly do this unless he himself sees something in it he never saw before" (83). At the same time, Cooley knew that teachers possess different sorts of temperament, and he concludes "Whatever else students do or

[15] Philip Rieff writes, "Abstractionist sociology expresses something more than a misguided labor to be a natural science; it demonstrates how far a great intellectual tradition has gone to pieces, to a point at which 'quality' is simply an archaic word for that which has not yet been quantified . . . As teachers, some of us, in the tradition of which Cooley was a practitioner, must keep open the possibility that sociology is a personal, normative—even transformative—discipline." Philip Rieff, *The Feeling Intellect: Selected Papers of Philip Rieff*, ed. Jonathan B. Imber (Chicago: University of Chicago Press, 1990), 311–12. See also Robert Gutman, "Cooley: A Perspective." *American Sociological Review* 23, no. 3 (June 1958): 251–56.

do not get they will always get your attitudes—as open-minded or dogmatic, adventurous or conventional, confident or suspicious, self-absorbed or appreciative of their personalities. For the last they are always grateful" (84). These are truly watchwords of the faith in teaching even as Cooley goes on to acknowledge that not all student are created equal: "The function of a college teacher divides itself into two not unequal parts; to help half his students educate themselves and to hinder the other half from getting easy credits. The crime side of life, with its suspicions, resentments and reprisals, is present in almost every class" (84).

Cooley's own self-deprecations about his vocation, that it is a "soft job" (83) or that faculty meetings are depressing because "I do not shine on these occasions" (84) reveal something about how he developed a teaching authority that was reflected no doubt in his work with students and the larger discipline of sociology. He embraced an obligation to teach students what he knew but not at the cost of what today would be described as "dumbing it down": "If you must choose it is better that students should not understand than that fine things should be made coarse in the telling. Let them become vaguely aware of something to divine and aspire toward" (85). What advice could be more contrary to the great transformation in the judgment of teaching that arose in the 1960s with students' evaluations of their professors? Where the line is drawn between a fresh performance and entertainment is not obvious, though how well students are taught can be measured by testing them. A teacher may be "hard" but admired because a student is able to distinguish between what was taught well and what was learned less well by factors unique to the student. This would require, of course, a student's own candor about his or her effort, the lack of which could be blamed on the teacher as well, thus echoing the "crime side of life" in its resentments and reprisals. Cooley saw how the navigation between faculty and student personalities was about an uncharted course where giving and taking offense is part of the nature of authority, however unconscious such a process may be. About students' character in this regard he noted, "College students are not the homogeneous crowd that some imagine. As in other societies, there is a dominant type or form that more or less imposes itself upon the whole, but underneath there are variants, many of them maladjusted and more or less psychopathic. In the eye of each, if you look for it, you may see an individual spirit, a self, often only partly at home with its fellows" (86).

Willard Waller, in a book that deserves to see the light of the present day, offered an acute sense of the psychopathic student in regard to the contesting of grades:

> "Rebellion and animosity flame into unpleasantness when student and teacher disagree over grades. Open argument is more likely to occur in colleges than in secondary or elementary schools, but it is found everywhere. Teachers need, for their protection in a situation, which would otherwise be very wasteful of emotional resources, techniques for avoiding or swiftly terminating arguments about grades. It is likely that neither argument nor persuasion will be very effective, for a student who writes a poor paper is probably unable to understand that such a paper is not a good paper, and besides he is emotionally biased . . . Students upon whom the pressure becomes severe may resort to cribbing, cheating, plagiarism, and other devices to beat the game."[16]

The dominant students at the most elite schools in America are deeply wedded to meritocracy. They face the prospect of competition in ways that long ago replaced collective entitlement with individual achievement. The "aristocracy of brains" has surely come to exemplify contemporary self-images of the young, at least in their attitudes about achievement, whether academic, social, or occupational. Every elite is established by not only a gatekeeper's discretion but by a factor even more relevant to those ambivalent about competition: Less room is available at the top than in the middle or at the bottom. In other words, the very top is also the top of a pyramid—with the fewest and most prized positions—referred to lately as the glass ceiling. The term "ceiling" is misleading because there is far less room above it than what is below, so that the more people who compete for those relatively fewer spaces, the more elusive those spaces are imagined to be. The term "glass ceiling" turns out to be code for accusations about race and gender discrimination aimed at present white-male dominated positions that will not be easily reduced to figure-head status without real risk to an organization's survival in a competitive world. Unlike the broader successes that have reduced discrimination in the rank and file of the professions, politics, and business, the creation of a more diverse pool

[16] Willard Waller, *The Sociology of Teaching* (New York: John Wiley, 1932), 360. On the same page, Waller also asked a question about the motivation for cheating: "There is a debate of long standing as to whether more students cheat in order to pass a course or in order to get a high grade." "Cribbing" is addressed by Ignace Feuerlicht in "Cribbing and Cheating." In *The Educational Forum* 17, no. 2 (January 1953): 199–201.

in the much smaller population *above* the glass ceiling will be regarded as nothing more than a symbolic victory undoubtedly leading to even greater pressure to disestablish hierarchies which is the unconscious motive to "break" or "shatter" the glass ceiling in the first place.[17]

Cooley noted the significance of universities as social institutions moving through a long transition: "Once the handmaid of the Church, they have now, as regards intellectual leadership, supplanted it" (87). Residues of church authority persist, in particular in Evangelical, Catholic and Mormon schools, but the new intellectual leadership that was fully emerging in Cooley's time now acts as the secular and social conscience of America, which helps to explain the notable lack of emphasis that most universities today have on the moral character of their inhabitants, moving from parietals to "hooking up" while inviting the full force of government to address the local moral vacuum that has been created in the meantime. That vacuum has brought with it chaotic efforts on the part of universities to mete out justice in cases of accusations about sexual harassment and assault, unleashing greater governmental oversight of private and public institutions.[18] Cooley also complained about pecuniary values, reflected in too much focus on athletics, and he lamented that "it is a peculiarity of American universities, incident to their expansion, that much of their activity resembles that of aggressive business. The administrative officers who have this activity in charge receive higher pay than the scholars, and in some cases appear more imbued by the commercial spirit than the academic" (89). This last observation and the truth of its insight have been further borne out in the obsession with "branding" in recent years. The faint, foul odor of the "commercial spirit" is not the real culprit. Rather it is the narrowing of

[17] Cooley was a consummate observer of these processes. See "Personal Competition" in *Sociological Theory and Social Research: Being Selected Papers of Charles Horton Cooley*, ed. Robert Cooley Angell (New York: Henry Holt, 1930). Higher education has expanded its numbers greatly in the past century, but Harvard, Yale, and Princeton have not grown proportionately larger by any means (even with greater representation of minorities), except perhaps in their democratic gestures of generosity in the development of massive open online courses (MOOCs), which reinforce the status of those who attend these places and those who do not. All democratic gestures reinforce status in very interesting ways. In the case of MOOCs, such generosity is not without the ambition to raise revenue. MOOCs are the loss leaders of elite institutions.

[18] Hyperbole and denial attend to the diminution of attention given to moral expectations in higher education, as if their discussion and debate are today entirely confined to the domain of religion rather than in continuing conversation with it. For one hardnosed illustration of the larger dilemma in an elite setting, see Nathan Harden, *Sex and God at Yale: Porn, Political Correctness, and a Good Education Gone Bad* (New York: St. Martin's Press, 2012).

ambition that makes administration superior to scholarship, as Cooley concluded: “The scholars may even seem a kind of caged and subdued animals whose exotic attractions are proclaimed and exploited by their keepers. Since they have, at any rate, less immediate power and prestige than the administrators it is difficult for them not to feel a certain inferiority, and men who appear to have executive ability (especially if they see no prospect of high distinction in scholarship) are under pressure to abandon teaching and research for administration, as they frequently do” (90). The corruptions begin first in the person, not the institution.

A Sociological Mission

In the final sections of this book on “Human Nature” and “The Larger Life,” Cooley advances in more general ways his philosophy of life. Some may regard his fairness to different views of human nature to be *too* fair, but who can avoid appreciating his way of formulating an opinion encouraging human improvement rather than railing against human failings. He also generously accepts the reality of the experience of many while expressing his admiration for exceptions to that reality: “It seems that in affairs the whole conception of merit is becoming transitive. That is, the ‘good man’ is not one who fits permanently into a function but one who is moving through and beyond it. Thus, he will do his present work the better, it is thought, because he sees it in perspective, and will also diffuse an outward and creative spirit. There is much in this, but I like also those who renounce ambition and cultivate gardens” (105). This generosity is one key to Cooley’s “transformative” sociology. He would hardly recognize the endless cultural imperatives endorsing the fulfillment of rights demanded by those filing endless grievances against invisible hegemonies that in their worst expression turn into conspiracy theories. All such claims have their source in individual paranoia which arises in forms other than class resentment. Cooley knew the character of such disturbances, but rather than fighting an entire lifetime against them, he saw the school as at least one place to mediate personality and social understanding not only more judiciously but even with humor (245).

The final forty pages of *Life and the Student* attest to what any close reader of Cooley’s more familiar works (e.g., *Human Nature and the Social Order, Social Organization, Social Process*) already knows. He understood the life of the group and the course of the future to be beyond the control of any one individual, however important individuals may become in their times and places. He eschewed vanity. He did not lend himself to this or that cause but knew that faith in something mattered to most people. World War I, still known in his lifetime as "the Great War," left in its aftermath a revulsion on his part for what preparing for war did to the youth of his time: "Such 'bolshevism' as I have seen among American youth was learned in the American army" (117). That aftermath did not make Cooley a pacifist, but it also alerted him to the vicissitudes of militancy in personality and ideology.

Cooley's final reflections are meditations on the bigger questions, in particular, death and the meaning of death: "No doubt my consciousness is involved with a physical organism and will cease when that decays, but while it lasts it shares in a continuing whole, made of a million such, and contributes to the common growth" (120). "Common growth," "common spirit," and "common life" are metaphors for Cooley's abiding faith in the ameliorative powers of human intention. He gladly praised Darwin as the greatest theologian: "Is not Darwin the chief modern theologian, since he made the largest and most fruitful study of how God works?" (121). Against prevailing moods, whether creationism or atheism, Cooley knew the irony in his assertion about Darwin, neither an accommodation to extremes nor an endorsement of a final judgment. Instead, he celebrated a sociological observation that gets short shrift in sociology today: "The world has always been full of conflict, hate, destruction; but beauty, love and power have grown in the midst of them" (122).

The subject of religion, which poses the bigger questions and where opinion divides characteristically between the sympathetic and hostile, is treated with Cooley's remarkable insight, an empirical intuition that is filled with prescience and respect: "Religion can hardly withstand science in the province of the knowable, and is likely more and more to avoid a conflict. But in the limitless regions of speculation and sentiment left open to them the religious inclinations will continue to expatiate and to build a world according to their needs" (124). A single meditation on Spinoza sums up Cooley's avoidance of entering into arguments about the existence of God. Instead, he asserts that "whatever leads one out into larger currents of life is an approach to God" (127), and that "our sense of a great life is hardly other than our sense of noble persons. To be loyal to them is to be loyal to God" (127). By contemporary standards of cynical sophistication among the higher educated, Cooley comes across as optimistic to a fault. His cheerfulness may irritate those who prefer an idealism rooted in the pain of existence, now more routinely described as the varieties of injustice (the popularization of "inequality" as injustice is only the most recent case in point) that pertain to that existence. Cooley did not discount such pain, but he saw in both Judaism (255) and Christianity (130) strengths against the pains and heartaches of life. He attributed these strengths to all humanity, even as he precluded the emergence of a universal religion (258). The catholicity of his thought was not Pollyannaish. Sociologists can never be real utopians.[19]

Charles Horton Cooley wisely observed that "Every fine idea is vulgarized in proportion as it becomes popular -- yet not altogether in vain" (12). His caveat is indicative of more than a generosity toward the leveling momentum of democratic life. Yet "not altogether in vain" could also mean something quite different, as Americans experience an opposite force where "fine ideas" are no longer the basis upon which popular culture is created. Leon Wieseltier captures the fate of elites that now peddle vulgarities exclusively:

> And to the inventory of alienating human productions one must add a good deal of American mass culture—for its transformation of a citizenry into an audience; for its hardening of an entire population toward the most obscene representations of violence, which we call entertainment; for its grotesque sexualization of an entire society, which has the effect not least of degrading sex, even dirty sex; for the mental passivity inculcated in millions of people who are helpless before its big and little screens, and who mistake screen-experience for experience; for the vicarious and self-estranged character of existences that are fascinated by celebrity culture; for the surrender of people's confidence in their own judgment as a result of its barrage of pseudo-expertise and pseudo-authority—I could go on.[20]

No single group, especially not intellectuals, public or otherwise, can reverse this fate as an entertainment-industrial complex competes successfully for the attention of the young who are more or less helpless to resist the consequences of the attention they give. Cooley stood at the precipice of an abyss into which would be dropped all the

[19] Russell Jacoby challenges the extraordinary insularity of academic Marxism and what should be considered, in contrast to Cooley, a naive (and I would argue murderous) ambition even though Jacoby may not think so. See Russell Jacoby, "Real Men Find Real Utopias," a review of *Envisioning Real Utopias*, by Erik Olin Wright. In *Dissent*, Winter 2011, 95–98. The American Sociological Association in 2013 entitled with oxymoronic precision its annual conference, "Real Utopias," following the election of Wright as its president, which confirms the real insularity of sociology itself.

[20] Leon Wieseltier, "Symposium, Part I: Intellectuals and Their America." *Dissent* 57, no. 1 (Winter 2010): 40.

idealizations of civilized behavior, turning the Great War into World War I. Disaster is always an opportunity for reform, but the aftermath of World War II cast doubt on all such idealizations, giving priority to creative destructions that appear to change human lives and its social configurations without the assurances of stability and what Cooley knew were the blessings and limits of freedom.

Cooley closes *Life and the Student* with reflections on religion, and in particular, Christianity. He criticizes a complacent church that does not do enough to reconcile abundance with sharing, today regarded as the sin of inequality. At the same time, in the final pages he also acknowledges the pitfalls of claiming to know what is better for others: "Too long we were taught that good will was the same as goodness. We now see that most evil is done by those who mean well" (135). Sociology could advance a better understanding of the difference between good will and goodness, which must begin first in the classroom, an ambition that embraces a close reading of human behavior in all its patterns and idiosyncrasies. Charles Horton Cooley still has much to teach us in that regard.

Jonathan B. Imber
August 17, 2014
Wellesley College

LIFE

AND THE STUDENT

Roadside Notes on Human Nature, Society, and Letters

by

CHARLES HORTON COOLEY

Professor of Sociology, University of Michigan

I. OUR TIME · II. READING AND WRITING · III. THINKING · IV. ART, SCIENCE, AND SOCIOLOGY · V. ACADEMIC · VI. HUMAN NATURE · LARGER LIFE

ALFRED · A · KNOPF · PUBLISHER · N. Y.

LIFE AND THE STUDENT

Roadside Notes on Human Nature, Society, and Letters

by

CHARLES HORTON COOLEY

Professor of Sociology, University of Michigan

To the judicious reader, this sequence of Emersonian observations and reflections comes with a two-fold claim, wholly aside from the general eminence of the author. First, the book contains an impressive amount of what can only be called wisdom, as distinguished from opinion, prejudice, theory, or dogma. Secondly, this ripe wisdom is conveyed in a prose firmly and beautifully entrenched in the classic virtues.

ALFRED · A · KNOPF · PUBLISHER · N. Y.

Part One

Our Time

Automobiles

WHAT a wonder of spontaneous adaptation is a town full of automobiles, charging back and forth (calamity if they meet) safeguarded by a few customs and a kind of intuition that comes with practice! Is it not so, essentially, with all our civilization? We live not by law or precept so much as by a sort of knack.

QUIET is recommended to the old, but I think that as we become more sunk in habit and less capable of renewal from within we may need more instigation from without—an automobile, let us say, which, God knows, keeps you bumping against other people in ways you never thought of.

I like this traveling by your own will and means, trusting to your own skill, liable to adventures.

The most retiring man, socially, may enjoy threading in a car the tumultuous traffic of a city. Since it is mechanical, not spiritual, he regards the other people only as natural obstacles and trusts to dexterity and resourcefulness much as in shooting rapids. It is indeed a sport not unlike canoeing.

On the open road, with the wind whistling in the superstructure, it is more like sailing.

How completely you are dependent for safety on the man in the passing car! You can only trust that if he were not a competent driver he would already have come to smash. Since he has survived he is presumably the fit.

I LIKE to go out on a wet and shiny night and watch the cars go by in an almost continuous double stream, each with its own peculiar interest of lights, equipment and motion. They make a fine spectacle of power, comfort and pleasure. It seems a good world: one looks to see it genially described, as London by Addison.

THIS childlike preoccupation of our people with mechanism is not such a bad thing; it keeps them innocently busy at least. Tinkering is a national pastime, and an interest in automobiles or gasoline launches almost a career in itself. There is a sort of culture in it, a common knowledge and faculty. Is any other part of our culture so much alive?

And how delightful to have such things to think and talk about—wonderful, shiny, oily playthings, fascinating in shape, color, texture and various harmony of motion; endearing in needing to be understood, coaxed, handled and taken apart.

We see that they are good.

ALL of our modern means of communication facilitate democracy by multiplying contacts. The automobile does this in rather a peculiar way, by causing all classes actually to rub against one another, as it were, on the open road. It brings many sorts of people face-to-face, and mostly under fellowship conditions. If you go on a journey you have constant occasion to give and receive courtesy and help. Every one sympathises with your adventure because everyone is doing, has done, or hopes to do something similar. He likes to help because it gives him a part in the game. You find that the American people are still a good-natured, easy-going, highly self-respecting, mildly adventurous, always humorous folk.

The inconvenience of running out of gasoline was nothing to the edification I had from the kindness of the country people near Chelsea. I should like to erect a monument to the Unknown Farmer, who has so often been good to me in every sort of difficulty.

IT is remarkable how rarely a stranger, known to be from a distant state and unlikely to return, is overcharged or otherwise taken advantage of. One does hot bargain with the garage men, but is fairly treated, and not seldom they will say "Oh you don't owe me anything," after giving you timely help or advice. Apparently the sort of men who make good in such trades are of a friendly disposition and habit. I have heard, however, that where the car and equipment are notably costly the charges are apt to rise.

I HAVE been in several small accidents and noticed that people did not lose their tempers. This amenity is probably not invariable, and yet American life trains in self-control because it is full of bumps, and no one is afraid of you. If you go into a rage the other man will laugh and say "Keep your shirt on!" In short anger is bad form. "Surtout, Messieurs, pas de zêle."

AUTOMOBILE travel tends to domesticate the whole country in every man's mind; his patriotism is enlarged without becoming less concrete.

I cannot agree that it is making us "an unstable, because nomadic, people." Is it not rather a flying shuttle that weaves the strands of our life into a broad and flexible fabric? It is not fixity that makes people stable, but possessions, hopes, contentment.

Strategy of the Youth Movement

ALTHOUGH the youth of our day are not so different from those of the past as they think they are, there is a distinct and perhaps lasting change in their situation. They have a new base and line of supplies. We have encouraged them to form social organizations of their own in connection with schools and amusements. Aided by telephones, motor cars and all the new appliance of intercourse, they have done this so effectively that they no longer depend for their patterns and mores upon adult groups and traditions, but have a continuous system of their own in which such things may grow and be perpetuated. They no longer get their contacts with the world and the past through a parent-ruled family, but in their own way and with their own kind, existing in a distinct milieu and a social heritage not sifted and censored by the mature. In the old novels you may see that the young rebelled indeed but that they saw it as rebellion, did not question that the elders were in authority, had no thought of a separate state. Now the channel of prestige is shifted, they flow in their own current, have their own orthodoxy, and in case of conflict it is the elders who appear ridiculous non-conformers to what youth regards as a matter of course. What can be done except to leave them to work out their own salvation by the aid of any advice they are inclined to take? While formerly whatever organization there was of the young was of either sex by itself, the new system includes both, associating in all possible intimacy. They discuss freely and apparently have the power to decide not only matters of religion and education but of sex conduct. The elders may still amuse themselves with property and politics.

Confusion and Continuity

IN a confused time there is a possibility of seeing life more largely than in any other, because no one tradition dominates thought and the need to choose opens our perspective.

A DISCONTINUOUS life breaks the fibre of our minds and makes shoddy of our thoughts. A haphazard society will generate unstable men. Broken homes and associations, broken habits, hopes and loyalties—few of us escape them and whole classes are thus demoralized. We strive, somewhat blindly, to avoid discontinuity or to heal its wounds.

Any notion of freedom that does not include continuity is illusive. We are free only as there is opened to us an orderly process of growth from what we are to something better.

Aside from any question of a second life, we need, especially after we pass middle age, a tangible future for plans and hope. In the past men have possessed this in various forms all of which gave them something substantial to look forward to beyond their own term. Among these were: their children and family line, especially if it had a permanent home with a hereditary occupation and standing; their neighborhood and local community, which was to almost every one before the industrial era, and still is to the majority of mankind, the most evident and cherished seat of a continuing system of life; their ancestral church and religious community, having sacred and beloved traditions intertwined with memories of birth, marriage, worship and death; and finally their country. All these a man might think of as living on after him, and he might, so long as his strength lasted, plan and work for them, perhaps forgetting in them his own precarious fate.

Few of these now appear to us with any assured stability. Except in the country the intimate neighborhood and community are all but gone, and even there it is broken.

The family has lost its permanent home and much of its inner solidarity; economic function is transitory; the church is questioned and neglected, our country is too far away for common uses. We splice the broken strands with such makeshifts as we find and trust that time will knit them up.

Certain sensitive people seek almost desperately to live in the sense of continuing life by cherishing the memories and heirlooms of their ancestors, the whole body and atmosphere in fact of the family and community which they inherit and hope to transmit. It keeps them feeling warm and safe, in out of the cold and desolation of an alien world.

THE castes of India and the peasant communities of Europe ensure to the individual a friendly and continuing group in which he can find secure life and self-expression. We try to recover this needful thing by insurance, by investments, by joining lodges, by reunions, by doing what we can to hold the family and the community together; but we shall hardly succeed until we get social union in our breadwinning occupations. Is not an occupation which is also a fellowship essential to a really human way of living?

THE ancestor-worshipping peoples of Japan and China are rich in continuity and think very little of the individual apart from the perpetual family group. Until their minds are unsettled by strange contacts they find in this all the religion they need.

In England the continuity of life used to be apparent in the establishments of the gentry, serving as a symbol for all classes. With us, it seems, the community must supply such symbols, which will be all the more reverenced as our life is individually shifting and precarious. In fact men more and more seek to associate their names and achievements with lasting institutions.

MANY contacts may or may not make for a larger growth of the mind. They will hardly do so unless one has the time and the disposition to brood over the material, philosophize and assimilate it.

THE characteristic moral problem of our time, not only in the family but in all our life, is that of substituting a free for a dogmatic discipline, of preserving integrity in the midst of a somewhat distracting increase of choice.

Shaky Bridges

WHEN I was a boy even intelligent people held that "free-thinking" about religion was dangerous and sinful—not without reason, since the church of that day was not built to stand the racket. What a confession of weakness in any institution to say "Do not think at will, it is not safe." It is like that sign formerly seen on old bridges, "Do not drive faster than a walk." Where unity is somewhat mechanical the ideas that sustain it are dogmatic, and must be uniform and sacrosanct, nothing else will preserve them. But a more inward unity, flowing from familiar intercourse and common experience, dispenses with dogma and thrives on discussion.

EVERY system, however free, must protect its vital parts. And it is only as people learn to distinguish what is vital from what is not that we can expect much increase of toleration. There could be little between Protestants and Catholics in seventeenth century France, because religious belief appeared at that time an inseparable part of the political order. Non-conformers were anarchists until they won, and then persecutors. Liberals forsook toleration because they saw it did not work. But we have an order based on self-expression, whose most vital part is precisely that freedom of discussion which we must protect at all costs.

I NOTICE that even the most generous and thoughtful of the Roman emperors, like Trajan and Marcus Aurelius, were convinced that freedom of speech and association must be restricted, just as in our time the same sort of people believe it should be encouraged. Our social order is flexible enough to stand it, to require it; theirs was not.

IN the new communication, in education and discussion, we have, what all previous ages have lacked, the means of free organization. It remains to see whether we have the intelligence and faith to use it.

"Our Complex Life"

WE talk, with reason, of the growing complexity of life, but there is also a trend toward simplification. We are being impelled to work out principles, general and flexible methods, instead of the cumbersome multiplicity of the past. An intelligent method is always simpler, more easily understood and surveyed, than one merely empirical. As we have reduced the alphabet to twenty-six letters, arithmetic and mechanics to a few elementary propositions, and have also arrived at solvent generalizations in the natural sciences, we may hope to do something analogous with our social processes. Even now our American democracy, as regards its principles, is perhaps the simplest large-scale system of life, as in its activities it is the most complex, that the world has seen.

There is a fair prospect of further merging our institutions of politics, economics, religion and education into a multiform unity.

THE disclosure of what appears to be universal evolution reveals system and hence simplicity in life, rendering us more and more capable of seeing it as a unified though multifarious process, in which our everyday experiences, if we will study them, appear as members of a whole.

Radicalism and Reaction

RADICALS and reactionaries are in alliance; each profits by the other; they mutually confer importance. Militarism and pacifism, Tolstoi and Bernhardi, go arm in arm; capitalism incites lawlessness in order to make its own rule appear necessary; the ascetic and the libertine are kindred spirits. These extremes are the common antagonist of moderate people who wish freedom and order.

As Darwin was able to predict a moth with a long proboscis from a flower with a long tube, so if you find an extreme view you may be almost certain that there is another extreme, of about the same length, to which it is an adaptation.

Weak minds loosed from old dogma take up with new folly equally dogmatic.

A "radical" movement, by the time it is widely known, has already become the convention of a sect, propagated by imitation and the ridicule of non-conformity.

Nothing more sheep-like than a flock of young rebels. Extreme thinkers are as a rule imitative, either directly or by opposition. Originality raises new issues.

What a boon to the reactionary is a revolution in another country! He no longer has to woo the public; it flies to his arms.

In our society the chief peril from the radical is that he affords a leverage for reactionary power. He is indeed partly a creation of the latter for this very purpose.

FORMALISM and anarchism are much the same, both consisting in a lack of assimilation between institutions and human nature. If the teacher and the children are in conflict it matters little which, for the time being, is on top.

PEOPLE think vaguely, and when they get hold of two apparently antithetical categories they find it easier and more amusing to sick them on each other, as it were, and make a fight out of it, than to think out their true relation.

WE wonder at the growth of fanatical movements, but it is more necessary that an idea should be active and communicable than that it should be reasonable. Or rather whatever releases activity along lines of desire will commonly appear reasonable. And any such movement gives the participant a sense of importance that the saner world may refuse.

VIOLENT revolutions are made by people who have had no chance to try out their ideas. Inexperienced minds think in formulas, and the formulas of a suppressed class are—what you might expect.

The Conservatism of Intelligence

THERE is nothing so conservative, in our day, as intelligence, and no radical so dangerous as he who blocks social research, experiment or discussion. How cheering to the radical is the fatuity of the people in power! Criticism of the present order, as regards any plan of general change, is weak and half-hearted. But when Chambers of Commerce, school boards or the like attempt to rule the press, coerce teachers and preachers or restrict popular discussion, they present their opponents, in place of this weakness and half-heartedness, with a strong and lively grievance sure to win the support of all disinterested men.

If conservative people were also wise they would promote social studies and the utmost freedom of discussion in the common schools. That these things are too difficult for school children is untrue. The difficulty is mainly in class-prejudice, and nothing will so surely prevent the growth of that as a common background of knowledge and mutual understanding. Why not have an education that shall teach the children of every class to see the point of view of every other? We trust to experience, which does wonders, but is too partial and often teaches the wrong things. A sound and honest social culture, acquired by all in the common schools, is the rational basis for democracy.

We can teach that habit of inquiring into facts which is the surest way to social intelligence and toleration. Without contradicting one's prejudices it goes back of them, gets him interested in fresh facts, and accustoms him to refer to facts his differences with others. It opposes stagnation, introversion, fanaticism, anything tending to a closed system of thought or emotion.

I notice a feeling among Americans that nothing American should be alien to them, that for patriotism, even for success, one ought to understand all phases of our life. And yet few carry out the idea. Why not proceed seriously in this direction, seeking sympathetic contact with the immigrant, the Negro, the radical, the striker, and re-solving not to be guilty of the illusions regarding their points of view that now prevail in other classes?

A TEACHER finds that extreme views do not survive comparative study. How many fanatic radicals and reactionaries have I seen thawed, as it were, by a little sociology. Not so much by reading or by hearing lectures as by finding, in discussion, what fellows of their own sort have to say on the other side.

Education and Religion

OUR FATHERS did wisely in separating public education from the institutions of religion; but there is a common and social religion that cannot be thus set apart. Social faith is much the same as religious, and if we gave to the young, in the family and the school, an adequate vision of their relation to mankind, they would not fail to extend this to God.

Nationality

THE self-consciousness of nations, like that of individuals, arises as they become aware of others, similar yet different, with which to compare themselves. It increases with the widening view of life in history, literature and commerce, and has reached the masses along with education and the cheap press. Although it is in its nature partial and gets its poignancy from the sense of difference, it is not inconsistent with cooperation and already makes the world a social whole in a sense it could not otherwise have been.

A social whole, to be alive, must be differentiated in emulous members.

AS individuals can develop a higher self only in an orderly society of their fellows, so with nations, patriotism and a world-order. Patriotism exists because there is intercourse among nations, and is brutal because that intercourse is superficial and unregulated.

One great use of a society of nations would be to make us more intelligently American.

THROUGH the democratic nation the spirits of men seek to unite in a lively and enduring whole, by participation wherein they may find release from ennui and mortality.

They have found this at times and in some measure. They will not cease to cherish patriotism, whatever arrogance or excess has stained its past.

IT is said that if all our thoughts were known we should have no friends. There could be no friendship, then, among nations, since the newspaper blabs everything. But in fact we know very well our friends do not always love us, and nations may agree in spite of the provocative press.

A WORLD state could have, as a whole, no poignancy of spirit like that of nations, because it would have no rivals. It might however have a lofty and not too placid self-consciousness. We may presume that inner troubles would in some degree compensate the lack of outer enemies.

A GROUP of self-conscious nations *may* destroy one another, but they have the option of organizing peace; blind forces have no such option, they inevitably clash. Nationality, however factious, is at present the only well-knit unit we have from which to build larger wholes.

American Patriotism

OUR American patriotism is for the most part not primarily local, like the European. How can it be when few remain in one place? The American sees America not as a household and a landscape, but as a place where you lead a certain kind of life: it is cheerful activity, fellowship, a chance for everybody, magnanimity, achievement.

IF patriots *were* patriots, if they were informed by the finer traditions of the country!—We are patriots much as we are Christians.

Our patriotism is in great part only a self-righteous orthodoxy. Like the Church it is taken over by the dominant institutions, and there is nothing too repugnant to its spirit to be inculcated in its name.

The timid patriot, like the timid Christian, is afraid of a rough-and-tumble handling of facts. He wants to take out an insurance policy on what he is used to regarding as sacred, to lock it up in a safe at the bank. He has no real confidence in its vitality; would protect it, protect it to death. He will use force to suppress opposition, or rather get others to use it for him, because he does not trust the freedom he is supposed to cherish.

PEOPLE say, "We must not be *too* tolerant," and call for suppression of what strikes them as dangerously wrong.

But tolerance does not mean indifference to wrong, or diminished vigor in combating it; rather, that the conflict should go on with all possible vigor, openly, fairly, and under such condition that the right may be free to prevail. It is a question of method.

There are three irrefutable reasons why views that seem dangerous, unpatriotic or otherwise abominable should be freely expressed. 1: Discussion is the only way to modify or control them. 2: It is the only way to mobilize conservative views in order to combat them intelligently. 3: They may be right.

Mass patriotism is made up of passions of the group self no more reasonable than those of the personal self, and less responsible, because there is less environing control by other selves. It easily runs into a tyrannical or destructive megalomania, like the undisciplined egoism of Commodus or Caligula.

There is no surer mark of a false patriotism than a forwardness to charge others with disloyalty. It is well to be critical of our compatriots at times, but always with an underlying faith in them. To accuse them of disloyalty as a mode of controversy or propagation is itself disloyal, since it is a cheapening of loyalty and a subordination of it to passion or interest. It is much like a jealous man arguing the infidelity of his wife.

Dr. Johnson, protagonist of loyalty and conservatism, observed that patriotism was the last refuge of a scoundrel. In any time of national excitement it becomes the first. Every base passion, every mean scheme, wraps itself in the flag.

Traits of Democracy

What shall we call our society? Democracy? There is no name: the fact itself has not been sufficiently perceived to have a name. There are democratic factors, oligarchic factors, autocratic factors, factors not comprisable in such categories, but enormously important to all of them, like the newspaper press. In general it is a society in which human nature strives hopefully, though somewhat blindly, for freedom and cooperation.

The test of democracy is getting every man's private self into the common game. The individual is mobilized; things are no longer done for him but through him; he is encouraged to be himself and to contribute in his own way; he may be persuaded but not dominated. And wherever men are treated as a crowd, where attempt is made to swamp individuality by propaganda, mass excitement or curtailing discussion; there democracy is in danger.

Democracy requires that we distinguish between leadership and domination. Let able men wield all the power they can, provided they do it in honest and open coöperation with the rest of us. But to persuade is more trouble than to dominate, and the powerful seldom take this trouble if they can avoid it.

What we need, you say, is an aristocracy of brains. That we need to be more guided by intelligence, wherever found, is most true; but if you mean that we are to look for this in a class, you are all wrong. A sound social intelligence is a function of the whole community. The higher influences reside more or less in all of us, though each of them more in some of us than in others. We must improve as a whole.

THE American, broadly contrasted with the European, has more belief that a good life for all is possible. The European fears life, puts little trust in common welfare and hugs his privileges. His keener sense of privacy is largely suspicion.

THE relative uniformity of American life, compared with that of Europe, is due to the historical background of the latter—a complex of ancient diversities, while America is new and assimilative. But since groups and provinces, like persons, have a natural pride in such differences from others as make them feel superior, we may expect a growth of local ambitions and claims upon renown to accompany the maturing of our order.

PUBLIC opinion is formed more by the interaction of characters than of arguments.

THERE are indications that women, as a group, are beginning to exercise some intelligent control over the course of fashion. If democracy can invade this seat of autocratic rule we may look for it anywhere.

EVERY fine idea is vulgarized in proportion as it becomes popular—yet not altogether in vain.

Immigrants

HOW poor American life would be without the immigrants— strangely colored threads from the fabric of the old world come to enliven our texture! One of the brightest joys I have is to know foreign-born students, to feel their eager response, favorable or otherwise, to our manners.

To make the best of an immigrant it is as necessary to respect his past as to influence his future.

We ascribe a long past to these "Orientals." But I talked with a Chinese boy to-day, and he seemed the newest thing on earth, fresh and unspoiled as a crocus, younger, I fancied, than a western youth of the same age, and more surprised at life.

Americanization

THE lady who cleans our house every two weeks arrives in her Ford car. She is of German birth and has a nephew recently come from Germany who is attending an Americanization class in the evenings. He is delighted with it, she tells us, and would like to do nothing else but go to school. The other night he came home and said he had been dancing. "But what would your teacher say if she knew you had been dancing at school?" "I danced with my teacher."

DRIVING to Grass Lake I picked up a boy of nineteen years who was just back from Florida, where he had been four months. He was born in Alsace and is a butcher by trade. He went to Florida in an Overland car, which he sold for $400, borrowed $400 more and set up a meat and grocery business, making about $1000. He got tired of it, however, sold out before the end of the season "while the selling was good" and bought a $1200 car in which he came home. Mud in Georgia and cold in the mountains gave him much trouble, he had to get hauled out and his car repaired so often that it took him twelve days to come back and cost $160. Now he has secured a job in Ypsilanti and his car was at Grass Lake getting a new set of valves. He has been back to Alsace and doesn't like it. I gathered that he found it slow.

Race

EVERY people seems coarse to every other. The savages on the Congo have standards of refinement of which we fall far short. They watch the white man and say "He is without background; he has not had the advantages of our society."

RACE is as difficult to discuss intelligently as God. Each sect or individual has his own idea, and all these ideas are bound up with inextinguishable emotions.

OF the hereditary traits of race, other than those physically apparent, nothing definite is known, because they do not manifest themselves in life apart from traits of the social heritage. We have, as it were, a single equation with two unknown quantities—x, equals race, and y, equals heritage. We can solve it for xy but not for x and y separately. Thus, in the case of the Japanese and the English, we can compare the two civilizations as wholes but not by factors. We do not know whether the Japanese x is the same as the English x or greater, or less, or merely different.

In refuting a popular view it is hard to refrain from asserting the opposite. Thus certain anthropologists, while showing that there is no proof of the superiority of one race over another, assert, or assume, that race abilities are equal—a gross *non sequitur.* This is a matter in which nothing is proved, and you are at liberty to believe what satisfies your working judgment.

It is not likely that the mental gifts of diverse human stocks are the same, and those stocks which believe that they have something of peculiar value are justified in avoiding mixture. Why not cherish the individuality of races, as we do that of persons, without raising the vague and invidious question of superiority?

Different race groups are apt to have intimate feelings, obscurely rooted in their different histories, which are antipathetic at close quarters. We can cultivate justice and understanding without falling on each other's necks.

The crowd of sightseers at Desbarats were a cheap looking lot compared with the Indians. If we are superior to them it is in some obscure capacity for discipline, fitting us better to carry the weight of institutions, a little tougher fibre, more continuity and system. In cleverness, sociability, dignity, they are at least our equals. They have companionable faces. I saw two who looked at each other *intimately.*

Contempt of another race is often one of those methods by which people suffering from a sense of inferiority seek to stimulate their self-respect. A white man, feeling that he is looked down upon by other white men, takes it out on the Negro. Where one race has formerly been enslaved by the other this attitude will be peculiarly lasting and arrogant.

It is upon crude minds that color and the twist of the eye work most virulently as stigmata to which hostile complexes may attach. Among intelligent people, not inflamed by economic opposition, like the students of various races found in our American colleges, a better feeling prevails. But since most minds are crude, I do not advocate the economic interpenetration of visibly distinct races.

"Race-prejudice" is not at all the same thing in the case of the Jew as in that of the Negro. The latter is a true caste pride, the heritage of slavery, defined by color and imputing an inferiority with no individual exceptions. It sees the race as a whole, is bent on keeping it in subjection, and abhors legal marriage or whatever else implies equality. The other, in America which has never had the Ghetto, is primarily individual; certain Jews are disliked and their traits attributed to a vaguely conceived "race." But as other Jews are observed to lack these traits they are regarded, except by a few fanatics, as people like anybody else. There is no history of caste, no dogma of collective inferiority and little repugnance to intermarriage.

C. A., whom I have known from childhood, was for many years in financial difficulties arising from the possession of tracts of unimproved real estate; to hang on to it and pay the taxes drove him to all kinds of shifts. He tells me that he has found the Jews, on the whole, the best people to deal with, that you get fairer treatment from them than from other lenders.

Anti-Semitism

I GATHER from anti-Semitic sources that while there may have been great and good Jews in the past they are all dead, or perhaps a few survive in distant lands. The Jews we know are obsequious and arrogant, superficial and inscrutable, intrusive and clannish, capitalistic and Bolshevistic, orientals without background, unscrupulous, competitious, commercialized; in short un-American and a menace.

What is peculiarly disgusting in the Jews is their prone ness to the so-called Christian virtues—humility, long-suffering, family loyalty, succor to the weak and the like—so repugnant to those sound principles of individual competition and the survival of the fittest by which we Christians are guided.

Eugenists

EUGENISTS seem not entirely consistent. When they are dealing with the poorer classes all is heredity; education can do nothing for these people; if environment is bad it is because heredity made it so. Poor stock! But in dealing with the degeneracy of the prosperous—luxury, decay of family life and failure to reproduce—is this due to heredity? Not at all! This is superior stock in a demoralizing environment. Let them be morally improved, coaxed to reform their habits and have more children.

Why ascribe other people's failings to nature and our own to circumstance? Can it be that social prejudice has something to do with these views?

If eugenists have not acquired an influence proportionate to their energy and the value of their idea it is perhaps due in part to faulty tactics. They are not team-workers. They have invented the specious dilemma "Heredity or Environment" and are trying to saw off the opposing horn on which sit History, Education, Social Work and other weighty interests. They do their best to show that if they are right all the rest of us must be wrong.

If heredity were so much more important than society as eugenists say, they might well ignore the latter. But apparently they do not believe it; they strive to influence the environment, neglect their own business for social propaganda.

What they really believe, we may infer, is that society has the power to control heredity, and should exercise that power in a certain sense.

One who reads the advertisements in the agricultural papers will see that there must be a firm belief that the offspring of hens who lay many eggs will do likewise, that good milkers will produce exuberant calves, and so on. On the other hand practical men who have to select boys put only a limited trust in ancestry. It seems to be settled empirically that human accomplishment is less predictable, more dependent upon obscure variations in both germ-plasm and society, than that of domestic animals. This is also sound in theory and renders a precise application of eugenics to human life highly problematic.

In spite of the fact that eugenists often seem so cocksure and one idea-ed that one hates to admit any agreement with them, it remains true that we shall not improve much unless we can have an intelligently selective birth-rate.

Team-Work

If there is anything of peculiar value in the fibre of the English-speaking peoples it is perhaps their spirit of team-work. This is not the same as the "solidarity" to which the French aspire; that is a more passive and uniform condition, based on likeness of sentiment in confronting the rest of the world. Team-work is rather a mode of action, a technique in group endeavor, a habit of playing the game. It involves agreement on an immediate purpose, mutual understanding and confidence, pleasure in merging yourself for the time in the group activity, respect for function and willingness to let the fittest lead. It may or may not rest on innate psychology, (some claim it as the birthright of the Teutonic stocks) but is in great part a social habit, a heritage from generations of voluntary and various cooperation, of love of sports and of group adventure by land and sea. Not always voluntary, either. I note in sea stories—say Captain Marryat's authentic tales of the time of Nelson—how the British seamen, brutally impressed, seem nevertheless to fall into their work with a certain good-will and self-respect, regarding the press-gang, and perhaps even flogging, as part of the game; but ready to resist real humiliation; ruled, withal, by honor and fellowship in battle and the hardships of the sea.

Of course men must always have shown team-work, it is the principle of society; you will find it well developed among the American Indians. Perhaps the Anglo-Saxons have merely been a little luckier than others in escaping the degenerative effect upon it of a coercive civilization. In any case we may take the word of Latin observers like Taine and Santayana that we excel in this trait, and may cherish it as perhaps the finest thing we have.

In our day team-work expands along with other things and tends to become universal, conscious and systematic, even in sports, which in some cases have grown to complex institutions. Organized play is carrying our forms of it around the earth, and we shall see whether we have any lasting superiority.

STENDHAL, in a curious passage written about 1830, invites the traveled reader to suppose himself taking at random one hundred well dressed Frenchmen passing over the Pont Royal, one hundred Englishmen crossing London Bridge, and one hundred Romans from the Corso. Then to choose from each of these hundreds the five men most notable for wit and courage. He discusses the traits that would be found in each contingent, and asserts that the five Romans would prevail over the five French or English, whether on a desert island, among the intrigues of a court, or in a stormy legislature, ascribing their superiority in part to their having lived a hazardous life under a bad government.

If you limit the struggle to merely individual combats, as he seems to, Stendhal may be right—for I do not know that national traits have changed appreciably—but I suspect that if the five English are allowed to form a team they will win.

OF two races one may excel in team-work and another in leadership, so that a mixture is stronger than either. Thus the Irish, although in the mass they have not held their own against the English, have furnished much more than their share of the great men of the British Empire. An American coach, noting that they excel in baseball, a game requiring chiefly individual quickness and skill, goes on "In football and basket-ball, games requiring a stronger team play, the Irish often prove to be star individual players around which the team is built. Their tempera-ment makes them good leaders, but they will seldom submit to being led . . . they are reckless, daring, resourceful and inspiring, contribut-ing to the team by their own brilliancy rather than by adding an extra amount of team strength."*

The highly mixed immigration that has come to the United States may well have given us a more capable human material than could have been drawn from any one racial stock.

THIS business of team-work by conference involves tolerance, good-humor and a certain practical sense. These highly educated and efficient men make large demands on one another's patience, talking somewhat ramblingly and egotistically, telling stories, sunning their individuali-ties. The "Anglo-Saxon" seems unable or unwilling to take in an idea except as he salivates it, like a boa-constrictor, with his individuality. Yet they get on, slowly, and seem to enjoy the process. A substantial friendliness underlies it all; there is a real human organism. Now and then a man will be found who has not quite the true spirit: he is a little inconsiderate, irritable, demanding, does not know when he has said enough or how to adapt himself to the general trend. Such a one is likely in time to be got rid of. Nothing more damaging to a man than to be held unfit for team-work.

AMERICAN life has always been such as to key the mind to process rather than rest, and this kinetic orientation is now extending from machinery and business into the sphere of large-scale social coopera-tion of every sort. There is arising a popular and practical psychology relating to leadership, dissemination, motivation of work and the like. We seem to be developing the practice, and in some measure the sci-ence, of corporate efficacy.

MR. BELLOC, an Englishman, remarks that "The American approaches and speaks to any man anywhere without previous knowledge of him.

* E. D. Mitchell, Racial Traits in Athletics, a series of articles published in The American Physical Education Review, Mar., Apr. and May, 1922.

Contact is established at once and as a matter of course." This is enormously strange, he says, to all Europeans.

I take it that this comes from our sense of active participation in a common life—as you would speak to a man you found playing ball with you, or working alongside you to put out a fire. Howells asserts that Americans are "all in the joke," and in like manner they are all in the general fun, quest and adventure of life. At any rate this is so usual that it determines the custom.

OUR social faculty outruns our knowledge. American life is moulded by strenuous cooperative men with more zeal in doing than clarity as to what ought to be done.

OUR inculcation of "salesmanship" seems to lack dignity, but does it not propose that understanding of the other man's point of view which is the condition of a more cooperative society? I do not see that, human nature being what it is, the study of persuasion can do it much harm.

HOW ardent for service are our leading citizens, in clubs of mingled membership! Outsiders deride and call it herd instinct, but this spirit, if intelligent,—and how, in this case, can it be otherwise?—is surely of no small value.

TEAM-WORK depends upon the vision of a common purpose. Those who conceive their own aims with a narrow intensity—the fanatical, the avaricious, the sensual—can never attain it. It grows by sympathy, by intelligence which sees the good of one in that of the group, by faith in the good sense and educability of men; above all it grows by practice, and there was never so much of that as now.

Social Mechanics

ANY social order is a formula of equilibrium among contending forces; from which, however, intelligence and love are not to be omitted.

THE secret of a stable society is simple: give all forms of energy a chance to express themselves within the system. Such disturbance as we have (not very serious as yet) comes from gross neglect of this principle.

TWO things needed in any system are freedom and stability. Are they compatible? Just in the measure that both are intelligent. An unintelligent freedom is anarchic and an unintelligent stability suppressive.

Neither of these can last long, and in fact freedom, stability and social intelligence make an indivisible trinity.

Classes and Culture

ALMOST everything in the way of culture, with us, suffers from *panmixia*, like the flavors of a boarding-house dinner. If we have fine minds they have not often been finely environed. We need enduring groups and traditions, which, however, need not be the invidious classes of the past.

There is no highly-developed man without highly-developed groups. If democracy meant sameness of life it would mean mediocrity of achievement. What is wrong is, not that groups are different, but that their differences are oppressive, invidious, have no high function. We are too alike in the spiritual things where we ought to differ, and too different in the material things where we ought to be, comparatively, alike.

There is nothing undemocratic about a class—scientific, artistic, academic, commercial, industrial—even though it have stringent and esoteric traditions, always provided that its aims are high and that it is accessible to the right sort of ability.

THE distinction between hereditary caste and functional classes is little understood in Europe, where they are historically almost the same, but they tend to differentiate in a mobile society, so that with us caste has been diminishing while functional groups, like the professions, have gained. We tend, apparently, towards open opportunity and a class system worked out through education and competition.

The Upper Class

COMPLEX societies, as they matured, have hitherto taken on a fixed structure of which an engrossing upper class has been a part. We are, perhaps, different; we have a flexible and fluent system which we hope to preserve; we *may* escape.

WE talk equal opportunity, but which of us is not striving to make it even more unequal than it is by getting privileges for his children? Moreover the privileged class strives as a body (though unconsciously) to increase its privileges. Yet we are sincere, perhaps, in wishing that things might, in general, be more equal, and, unless our own advantages are at stake, are not unwilling to do something toward this end.

Nothing more occupies our minds, after the accumulation of wealth, than how to prevent its dispersion when we die. The science of investment, wills, trusts, insurance, educating our children in the technique of conservation—if a hereditary plutocracy does not emerge it will not be our fault.

"There is no class-consciousness among our leading men; they are just individuals, abler or luckier than others, but all in favor of equal opportunity."

This is not far from true, and yet there is in effect if not intention a dominant upper class which controls our system in its own interest. A business group, united by common ideals, practices and limitations, having the machinery in its hands, does not need class-consciousness in order to be an aggressive whole, destructive of other types and tendencies. It is enough that its members should strive ahead in their own sense. And even if equal opportunity to win in this game were attained it would only establish the game.

Class-consciousness in other classes is desirable as a check on the dominant class and as a means to a richer variety of ideals and leadership. The learned professions, especially, have too little corporate ideality and pride, are far too much the mere hired men of capitalism.

Responsibility goes with power, and the blame for crime, vice and misery belongs chiefly to the educated and well-to-do classes. Some try to meet it by knowledge and service; the most either do not think of it at all or justify themselves by vague theories of "the survival of the fittest."

It is rare to find among the well-to-do any sense that we eat, after all, from a common platter, and that, in a given state of production, the more one consumes for his own use the less is left for others. We act as if what a man takes were no one's business but his own, and those who swallow five times the average share are eager to equal those who engorge ten or twenty times.

It is partly to avoid consciousness of greed that we prefer to associate with those who are at least as greedy as ourselves. Those who consume much less are a reproach.

Is there not a kind of emptiness in the upper stories of society, too much room and equipment for the life that inhabits it? Think of the deserted streets in the richer quarters of town, the large separate houses with few or no children, people who do not know what to do with themselves.

It is characteristic of our society that the strong do not much cultivate external inequalities: that our use of wealth and power is somewhat deprecatory. Democracy of feeling is expected of us, and if we do not have it we usually simulate it. It is not at all as in countries—if there are any such left—where caste is a declared and accepted fact.

The expression of power in manners and dress is more invidious than the inner reality, and we do not commonly grudge a man superiority if he consults our self-respect in the use of it.

It is a real mark of democracy that our frivolous people of the wealthy class seek general publicity in the newspapers. It shows that they have no true caste sentiment, do not even pretend to have, for nothing is so vulgar from a caste standpoint as an appeal to the general public.

Class Magazines

The friday morning mail, a splendid magazine, yours for five cents, read by all business men and most college students, having a fabulous income from advertising, is a mirror of our state. It has amusing stories, informing articles, illustrations, cartoons, all good of their kind. Our civilization is exalted, the capitalist admires himself and his world. The rule of business men is assumed to be natural and beneficent; insurgency, if mentioned at all, is discredited in the articles and derided in the cartoons. The young are assured that all have an equal chance and that enterprise and virtue will gain them riches and power. Poverty is either a myth or a just punishment. You would scarcely learn of a strenuous and high-minded labor movement, winning human conditions of living inch by inch in a long struggle against the inertia, greed and detraction of employers. The atmosphere is that of an energetic, good-natured, naïvely exploiting class, by no means hardened or sordid, but superficial and with little sense of social responsibility. The American business man is, typically, a good fellow who knows only one sort of ideas and has been brought up to believe that virtue is measured by what you can get. A class of such men, possessed of power and driven by emulation, can and do impose their own spirit upon society at the expense of democracy, community, beauty, fulness of life or anything else with which it may conflict.

Certain magazines specialize in exciting ambition by biographies of success. This is healthy so long as the suggestions are moderate and practical but easily becomes delusive. It also intensifies the actual narrowness of ideal, and has the effect of upper-class propaganda in that it glorifies successful men of the prevailing type.

I DO not wonder at the Socialist belief that the press and the business class are in a conspiracy to conceal social truth. They could hardly do it more effectually if they were—less effectually indeed, since the surest way to deceive others is to believe in your own good faith.

The upper class is narrow-minded because the press gives it only one kind of social ideas; and the press does this because it knows that the upper class, being narrow-minded, doesn't want any other kind of ideas.

The Handworking Classes

IT used to be thought, perhaps rightly, that education would make the handworking classes discontented. But in our time they get suggestions of discontent by many channels, and the only thing that can give them a stabilizing outlook is a social education that will teach them how they may better themselves, as a class, by moderate and continuous endeavor, rather than by spasmodic and subversive outbreaks.

I GET my most hopeful impressions of democracy from intelligent handworking men, from farmers, teachers, impecunious students, from almost any source except the more opulent commercial and professional classes.

A locomotive engineer called upon me yesterday—a big, frank intelligent man about forty—and talked concerning a plan for more democratic control of business organizations which he and other union men were trying out in a cooperative coal company. He has been working for twenty years on such matters, he says, and has never received a cent for it; it is his avocation. He is unmarried, has a library and is something of a scholar. I have come across not a few men of similar initiative and public spirit, some of them immigrants, all from what many would regard as an inferior class.

THE struggles of the ill-paid classes are on behalf of society as much as those of soldiers at the front. They are holding a line—a standard of self-support, loyalty, health, decent rearing of children and the like—the breaking of which would impair our civilization and injure every class. Perhaps I should rather say that they are striving to establish a line which is dangerously lacking at present.

We ought, then, to stand by them not from pity but as comrades.

LOYALTY and service flourish only in congenial association. We shall never have contented and efficient workers except as members of occupational groups, continuous, well-knit and responsible, such as we now have in properly organized professions, bearers of tradition and standard, guaranties of security, self-expression and a human life.

YOU write "self-expression" in contemptuous quotation marks, as if it were a fad. I can only say that I have found self-expression to be in fact, as it is in principle, the heart of life. I believe that all might have it, intend to have it for myself, and to do what I can to get it for others.

Class-Conflict

CLASS-CONFLICT in America is a multiform, confused and shifting affair, hard to follow in its processes and outcome, not at all a sharply defined struggle between capitalist and proletarian. Class allegiance is loose and often transient. The stronger individuals tend to work from less privileged groups into more privileged, the stronger groups acquire privileges, everybody treads on the weak. And with all the confusion and injustice there is an underlying stability, because energy finds, for the most part, a hopeful outlet within the system.

WE claim to be good sportsmen, and it would seem that our social contentions should be carried on in that spirit. This is sometimes the case as among members of the same social class, almost never as between classes. When the opponent is the immigrant, the Negro or the industrial worker the tactics are arrogant, ruthless, often treacherous, as in the use of spies and provocative agents by the rulers of industry.

IT is a cherished illusion of the business class that they stand for law and order. I have observed that when alarmed they usually blink, condone or applaud the lawless use of force on their own side, and that the large-scale, well-considered and successful violations of justice and freedom are mostly in the interest of "capital." The anarchism of labor is more shocking, less dangerous.

THE vague and groundless fear of economic revolution that from time to time attacks the privileged classes of America appears to be due to ignorance, timidity and a bad conscience: perhaps also to the propaganda of those who have an interest in giving the public mind this direction rather than one more troublesome to themselves. What makes the alarm of the propertied class rather ridiculous is that they do not see the strength of their own position: it is an elephant trembling at a mouse. The ignorant are always afraid of the wrong things.

ANY theory which makes it appear that the class on top have a natural right to be there is eagerly accepted by that class. As, for example, that the process of making money is a "survival of the fittest"; that opportunity is equal to all; that it does more harm than good to try to help the poor; that the successful belong to a distinct and superior race; that "intelligence tests," in which the children of the well-to-do generally excel those of the poorer classes, are tests of native ability alone and not also of social advantage.

THERE has always been a dominant class of one sort or another. At present its rule is less assured, less accepted and less harsh than commonly in the past; nevertheless it absorbs wealth, controls institutions and presses relentlessly upon the weak at the bottom. I see no prospect of its disappearance, but some of its being curbed by other classes and by a more intelligent public opinion.

As war is a waste so, for the most part, is economic strife between classes. It, also, is based mainly on ignorance. The hope of our civilization is not in class-conflict (though that is for the time being inevitable) but in the social enlightenment of all classes and the growth of intelligent processes of cooperation.

Rural Physiognomy

FOURTH of July celebration at X. The impression a town-dweller gets from the rural crowd is one of un-couthness and a slight imbecility. They dress any old way, carry themselves loosely and seem vacant and purposeless. Many have physical defects, and few appear altogether sane, sound and self-possessed. You note that naïvety and unconscious exaggeration of themselves due to lack of social discipline. Each abounds in his peculiar sense, and many would shine on the stage as types. In fact, however, these are good people, self-respecting, even proud, remarkably honest, and more intelligent than they appear. In this vicinity they are nearly all native Americans of old stock, speak good English and have most kindly manners. No doubt the level of ability has been lowered by selective migration to the towns. At least one gets from them no such impression of vitality, force and promise as I got, for example, from the crowd of foreigners at Revere Beach near Boston.

COUNTRY faces are more fully characterized than city faces, have less of that social mobility and pose, that visible habit of dressing their expression and bodily carriage for the eyes of other people, which you see in the urbane classes. They have perhaps no more individuality, but it is of a different sort, more naïve, the individuality of isolation, as contrasted with the organic and sophisticated individuality of towns.

Progress?

Is progress a fact? Evolution is, and if you think evolution is worth while it is progress.

Experience shows that when we intelligently try to move in a desired direction we can do so. What more can we ask?

Mankind as a whole, like the individual, enquires "Can I make my life more satisfactory than it is?" And the answer is up to us as it is up to him.

THE *process* of progress—the hopeful and constructive life involved in building up what seems to us a better state of things—is more surely good, perhaps, than any goal we attain.

That the race will be happier a century hence for our exertions may be true; I hope so; but I find no great incentive in it. I live in the process and find my own little plans and hopes enough. Perhaps, however, I should not be content if I could not, at certain times, raise my eyes and see these plans leading out into a larger picture.

I NOTICE a disposition among thoughtful men to deprecate the idea of progress. It is perhaps a reaction from the preoccupation with inventions and material growth, an insistence that what is worth while must be now—or never—a protest against neglecting the human present for a future that never arrives. I agree that we should make the most of life as we go along, but I see no reason why we should not regard also the general movement of things, find that more or less good, and try to make it better. I strive to improve my own state; it would be unnatural not to extend this process to humanity.

WHAT we want, I suppose, is a developing, productive life for each man after his best kind, and for each group likewise. Life as it is is in great part confined, stagnant, futile. We have constructive energy, but it works in narrow channels, for a small class and to rather low ends.

DURING my lifetime there has been, in America, a persistent though irregular growth of personal freedom and humane organization. And I remember how my father used to contrast the comparative amenity of my boyhood, especially as regards the conduct of schools, with the brutal conditions of his own.

Part Two

Reading And Writing

Books and Persons

AN intelligent reader goes slowly when he feels that each word has its peculiar and essential force. He watches the author. We *want* to make out personality, and if there is the least trace of it imagination is excited and puts forth guesses, we become clairvoyant. We want the author himself, as an explanation, a guaranty, a vehicle for the thought. And we find him in his choice of words, in the movement of his sentences, in the attitudes and habits of feeling implicit in what he says, in a hundred signs not less telling, to the sensitive reader, than the visible and audible man.

I know one who can keep children laughing with only a droll look now and then, and so there are authors who keep you amused and expectant of humor though they but rarely deliver it. We act on others not so much by what we explicitly do as by inciting their imaginations to work in a certain direction.

IF a man writes thoughtfully he will not fail to impart his spirit, however slight the matter may seem. From Gissing's sketches of travel By the Ionian Sea I get a deep and moving sense of his personality: just how and where it is conveyed would be hard to say. Like everything he wrote it is interfused with a fine kind of pride.

I LOVE good books of travel, with a real atmosphere of strange places, but I find very few of them. I go to the library to find a book on Italy, and try one after another without satisfaction. The trouble is, in general, that there is nobody at home. The writer forsook himself when he wrote, he was not heartily in it, the works are perfunctory, not containing any full stream of spirit to float you away into new regions of life, thin, colorless, hardly existent.

IF I think of certain academic men and ask whether they would be interesting in literature, I see that they would not. They are too anxious about being something else than simply men, not firmly enough poised. They see themselves in the light of some phase of opinion, as literary or scientific. A solid carpenter is better, he seems more human, less institutional.

I FIND Henry James's early letters from Europe less interesting than Mr. Dreiser's rather crude book A Traveler at Forty. There is no stark personality in them; it is impersonal culture and craftsmanship; he is lost in his art.

A CHOICE spirit defines itself in great part by what it avoids—the trite, the superfluous, the insincere, the immoderate—and may hold our attention more by this than by positive matter. The harm of a needless word is not so much in wasting the reader's attention as in impairing his confidence in the writer.

HOW grateful are limits! In a tale of Jane Austen you may be sure there are no social problems, no intellectual puzzles, no harrowing emotion. It is all well within your reach, clearly imagined, spirited, witty, exquisite of its kind. Second-rateness consists largely in slopping over, in not drawing a firm line around your picture, in doing poorly what you ought not to do at all.

HENRY JAMES is one of the authors that I can read with delight over and over again. He has a whole-hearted joy in his work and exhales a joyous though much rarefied atmosphere, wherein, if you can breathe it, you may recreate your mind with exploration of a subtile and enticing world. In his earlier books he has also a light ingratiating humor and a caressing flow of speech. That his range is limited, that there is no passion in him except the passion for literature, is perhaps an added charm; he invites you into an enclosed garden where nothing lives but literary grace and psychological intelligence.

I READ the French moralists—de la Rochefoucauld, La Bruyère, Pascal—not so much for the value of their ideas, however great that may be, as because I like the company of men who are interested in such ideas.

Character

WHAT is it that makes most books unsatisfying? Is it not lack of character, of reality? A certain opportunism, aiming at the market rather than at truth? The writers seem too much applicants for favor. They offer, for the most part, not solid individual contributions but voices in a chorus, each taking the key from the rest but striving to be a little louder or clearer or sharper or in some way consciously distinct, so as to be sure of being heard. What we want, apparently, is to hear voices that are *unconsciously* distinct, not anxious about being heard, speaking from a quiet background of normal life and expressing without strain a natural and interesting self.

COMPOSURE is communicated by the gesture of a book, a way about it that makes one feel that the writer is in no hurry, is not trying too hard and enjoys his paragraph as he makes it. We wish him to create a world of his own, joyous and serene, and then make it our world. He must be bold and unique for us, because we are to enter into him. He should live the most satisfying life he can, so that we may see how it is done. Apology is as distasteful as it would be in an actor, it destroys our illusion. One must be in quiet and secure possession of some sort of a homestead in order to be worth while in literature.

The Book and the Sentence

THE book and the sentence are like the state and the man; too much system in the whole enslaves the individual. A spontaneous observation has a certain life of its own, "the hue and flavor of the thought," which is apt to be lost by marshalling it in lock step with others. Let it appear for the moment in its own right, a simple and natural fact.

ONE'S thoughts unite into a book for mutual encouragement and protection. Each of them is bold like a man among friends. One says things with confidence that he could not say at all if they stood alone.

Form

WHAT is this Form about which so much is written? Should it not mean a living and palpable whole in the artist's mind, intimately his by its growth in and through him? And if he can adequately deliver this his work has form. Form as a separate thing, as a container for something else, is formalism. All original masterly work has form; second hand or uninspired labor can never create it. It is what Goethe meant when he wrote "I will rest no more until it is no more word and tradition but living conception." *(Lebendiger Begriff.)*

Freedom in Books

FREEDOM is one of the subtlest, most engaging and least attainable by effort of literary attractions. When we read for pleasure we hate all bounds save those of art and like to feel that the author will say anything that suits his humor. Montaigne has it, and Lamb, Emerson, Thoreau, Whitman, George Borrow and many others—Shakspeare more than anybody. Literature is not written in a uniform, although Buffon wore his dress suit when composing his Natural History. Some have freedom who have little else, but if they are unaffected—as they must be to be truly free—they are not without interest.

WRITERS who are out to demonstrate a theory—Herbert Spencer, Taine, Buckle, Marxians, Galtonians and the like—are not for me. They see nothing freshly and do not help me to. You might as well listen to an agent.

HOW it sickens one to feel that the author writes from a sense of duty! "In treating this branch of the subject. . . ."

I think we require the light touch more as we grow older and have less moral ardor. We read Herbert Spencer at twenty-five but prefer Montaigne at fifty.

THE thoughts a man thinks for his own use, without the sense of an audience, are usually his best, because they are the freest and most characteristic. They speak not *to* the reader but *for* him: he adopts them as his own. Much good matter is spoilt by lack of courage to let it stand as it was naïvely seen and felt.

Almost any naïve and lucid account of experience is pleasing, because it takes us out of ourselves. The trouble with most naturalistic writing is that it is not naïve: it conveys not only nature but the intention of the writer, which is apt to be a bore.

AN elaborate style has perils like those of an elaborate house. It commits the author, by habit and the expectation of others, to a special and costly way of living, which will become a burden when he loses the wish or the power to keep it up. Such writers often grow stale and formal with time, as was somewhat the case with Gibbon.

THERE is a kind of writing which sets the reader on a track and holds him to it till the end of the piece. Macaulay would be a model for it: attention is spurred by rhetoric and the line of thought made cogent by connection and illustration. No thoughtful man is convinced in this way. You will never get him unless you induce him to convince himself, as you may perhaps by such suggestion and deference as will lead him to see the matter from your point of view.

It is said that in learning a language one gets a new soul, and certainly a strange tongue seems in a peculiar way to take one out of oneself and rest his spirit. It is somewhat as if we were children again, enjoying the first surprise and adventure of words. At least so I have found it, and this, as much as anything, has kept me puzzling over dictionaries.

Diary Books

The method of making a book out of spontaneous thoughts set down in a diary has always been in use, but never more candidly than by Emerson and Thoreau. The result is naïve, human, full of variety and special color. There is nothing perfunctory, all is real. In Emerson almost every sentence is an anecdote, a picture or an epigram. No writing could have less waste; it is all diamonds and no setting.

On the other hand, if one's mind is desultory this method does nothing to correct it. The diarist is apt to reiterate the same idea without knowing he does so, and without seeing where his thought needs development. Emerson and Thoreau did not wholly escape this.

It is difficult to record thoughts naïvely when you know you may use them in a book. Only secluded spirits with a settled habit of writing to themselves can do it, and they not perfectly. There is perhaps nothing so noble of this kind as the thoughts of Marcus Aurelius, who did not expect a reader.

Emerson and Thoreau are remarkable for the directness, with no veil of art, with which they print intimate thoughts just as they entered them in their journals. They can do this without offence because their minds were habitually sincere, aspiring and free from turbid passions. La Bruyère may have had a good deal not fit to print. Montaigne is different in another way; his thinking seems conversational rather than private, not diary-stuff at all, always intended for a public.

Emerson should be read in youth. His boundless hope and his call to self-trust are congenial then. Later, when you have become disillusioned, sceptical and lazy, you may find his exhortations a little tiresome, his thinking inexact, and his optimism not wholly verified. I wore out a set of his works when I was young, and even now I carry about a thin book of extracts to which I resort when I need to find a little more glamour on life.

A VIVID but fragmentary writer, like Emerson, influences us more than we are aware of. The thought takes root, but as there is nothing to trace it by we forget where it came from. You may find in him much of what is essential in Nietzsche, Bergson, William James, John Dewey.

IF a man feels that his life is wonderful, and if he is reflective withal, he wishes to make a record in order more fully to realize and preserve it. So Pepys overflowed with wonder and delight that he should be a part of these great events, "himself not least but honored of them all." And no doubt he loved to reread it. "A man," said Doctor Johnson, "loves to review his own mind."

I think also that our Pepys was something of a psychologist, one who felt a need to penetrate beneath the surface of things and reveal true motives, both his own and those of others. We say he is naïve when he points out his own prevarications, but it takes more than naïvety to know yourself as well as that.

THE reading of diaries, memoirs and such like simple records of the past is peculiarly wholesome to a thinker; they give him a human perspective by which to judge sanely of a plan or a theory. How does it fit into the picture?

A PENSÉE is best when strongly felt and wholly spontaneous and of the moment, with the individuality and naïve detail that such thoughts have, yet not without some large outlook. It should be between the thinker and God; whatever suggests another audience impairs it.

A BOOK of paragraphs is a five-and-ten-cent store where you can enter with the assurance that you will not be urged to buy more than you can afford.

Literary Selves

NOTHING so interesting as a self in action. I have to read many hundred student papers. When a writer says "I" and goes on to tell of a bit of his life that meant something to him, tells it as if he were the first man on earth to live it, I find myself taking notice. No matter how trite it is, if it is fresh to him I enjoy it. A spirit of living is the most communicable thing in the world, and the most worth communicating.

An artistic personality is a special sense of self and a special manifestation of this to others which one develops in the practice of any art. It is both more and less than his usual self, and is, in fact, the original work of art of which all his other works are children. He needs it in order that he may realize himself, for a given purpose, with the stability and assurance necessary to consistent work. It has something of the nature of an institution, like the church, through which a phase of the spirit is organized and effectuated. It mediates between human nature and life.

Every person of any distinction of character, especially every artist, and above all every literary artist, forms his own portrait for us out of our susceptibilities, by awakening those that correspond to his self-expression. We offer ourselves like a piano, or rather like a whole orchestra of possible notes, for each man to play his own compositions upon, and it is this evocation, in a distinctive pattern, of ourselves, that communicates his character. He comes alive in us.

A writer builds his literary personality by the habit of intimate self-expression, supported, usually, by the sympathy of an audience, which stimulates, selects and develops capacities of which he would otherwise have been unaware. As a rule he must have at least an occasional hearing or remain vague and abortive. Indeed I think that some sort of interaction always takes place, although if the need of expression is urgent one may write with no immediate sense of an audience, like Marcus Aurelius in his Meditations. He would probably have written no meditations if he had not been, in other directions, a practiced writer and speaker, and so developed a literary self.

Learning to know and express a presentable self is a thing so difficult and precarious that an artist does not accomplish it except in certain phases of his personality which choice and appreciation determine. These flourish like the one shoot of a dark-growing plant that finds the sun. His artistic personality is a special and abnormally developed part of his real self, genuine, no doubt, but also a pose. Thus no one has the freedom of an artist except within certain limits, but these are much wider for some than for others. You feel that you know only a small and elaborated part of Walter Pater; of R. L. Stevenson more, though by no means all, while in Goethe the man and the artist seem hardly distinguishable.

A MAN of scope, who writes rather to develop himself than to please the immediate public, is likely to find, as Goethe did, that each step in his growth is resented by his friends, who have formed from his previous works an ideal of him which they hate to have disturbed.

IT is said that the greatest writers are not personal, that we do not feel personality in Dante or Shakspeare, that true literature is drawn from impersonal depths which belong to the common human mind. This, I think, begs the question by assuming that personality is something superficial. Dante and Shakspeare are never more unique and individual than when they are speaking from depths—we do not doubt which it is that is speaking.

There is, no doubt, a kind of gossiping egotism, which some call personality, that is found chiefly in minor writers, though also in Sterne and Horace, in the autobiographical writings of Goethe, and even in two or three of Shakspeare's sonnets.

AS to that question whether the actor ought to *be* his part, I take it that the rôle is an artistic self which must be developed from the real self of the actor, but gains in the process a somewhat independent and mechanized life. While acting he must both be this self and at the same time, in his more usual self, survey and control it.

Egotism

WE do not care to reread what we have thought with a purpose; but the naïve, self-colored, intimately cherished meditations of that shy and arrogant dreamer that was oneself, are not without a charm.

SELF answers to self, and we love a congenial egotist. We love him because by sympathy we can and do expand our own spirit to the measure of his. And if we hate an egotist it is because there is something in his ego to share which degrades or insults our own. We do not care to wear another man's dirty shirts.

This is notably true in the so-called spiritual life. What makes Augustine great is, in large part, his frankness in depicting his own sins and struggles: he is thus dramatic, imaginable, a living companion in the Christian way. The men of moral power are nearly all egotists; as St. Paul, Luther, Dante, Tolstoi, Nietzsche, Carlyle, Emerson, even Jesus. On the other hand is there anything so nauseous as the affectation, grossness or self-complacency of a pseudo-spiritual egotist? If half the ministers were suppressed the Church would be more respected.

WE may like in literature an egotism that would bore us in conversation. In the former case we can choose the time and manner of identifying ourselves with it.

I DOUBT whether any writer has suffered with the public in the long run on account of egotism, as such. The younger Pliny published his own letters, and nearly every letter seems selected, if not written, to illustrate or suggest some virtue of the author—his generosity, magnanimity, moderation; his reputation for eloquence, humane culture and practical wisdom. "Nothing," he confesses, "so strongly affects me as the desire of a lasting name; a passion highly worthy of the human breast, especially of one who, not being conscious to himself of any ill, is not afraid of being known to posterity. It is the continual subject, therefore, of my thoughts, 'By what fair deed I too may raise a name.'"* Such a book would be ridiculed now and no doubt was then. Yet as he seems an honest sort of man, who really had these virtues, posterity likes him all the better for that kindly yearning to have them appreciated. It is a winning book, and one only regrets that there are not ten volumes instead of two.

And yet . . . this self-complacency . . . I wonder whether his wife admired him as much as he would think she did?

THE truth is that egotists (as distinguished from egoists) are people whose selves are conscious, social and expressive, and for that reason likely to be more human and less ruthless than those that have never come out into the common life. If a man lacks a streak of kindly egotism, beware of him.

A DOG differs from a cat in having a looking-glass self. He is interested in what you are thinking of him, studies your eye, acts little plays for your approval. A cat cares for you only as a source of food, security and a place in the sun. Her high self-sufficiency is her charm. She is an egoist; the dog, sometimes, an egotist.

* Book V, Letter 8, Melmoth's translation.

FREE spirits usually value self-expression too highly themselves to complain of it in others. "It cost me nothing," said Goethe, "to let others pass for what they were, yes, even for what they wished to appear to be." Those who censure it are sometimes moved by envy of a freedom they dare not emulate.

SOME of our young and radical writers seem lost in curious forms of egotism, interesting as detail, (I by no means condemn them) but without liaison or large significance. They need a whole to give them alignment and function.

WHAT is truly repellent is an egotism that has not confidence and gusto enough to put itself bravely forward, but is more or less clandestine or affected. This is odious because our own self is attainted by a beginning sympathy with it.

OUR day inclines to a complete frankness of self-expression. We feel that if one has anything worth sharing he cannot say it too intimately. And since it is, in the nature of the case, a part of himself, why try to make it seem something else?

THE chief objection to the frequent use of "I" is that it is always a vivid note, somewhat perturbing because it awakens a self in the reader, harsh if it fails to be harmonious. There is something contentious in the sense of self; it is born of opposition; and when a man says "I" emphatically he, as it were, puts a chip on his shoulder, he starts a quarrel with us, unless he makes us feel, at the same time, that we are on his side.

MANY authors therefore avoid it (Walter Pater, let us say) not for lack of self-assertion but to get a quieter, more impersonal atmosphere, more suitable, possibly, for delicate perceptions. And there are others who urge and exploit their egotism, (Hazlitt, perhaps) because they know that readers like it as a stimulant to their own self-feeling.

There is indeed a school of popular writers (mild fellows probably) who assume a truculent and iconoclastic egotism, perhaps in order to gratify vicariously the suppressed selves of their public.

IT is a superficial question, as to whether literature should be personal or not. All is personal in substance, the important thing being the sort of personality, not whether it is overt or masked.

The use of the first person concerns chiefly a writer's own feeling. To avoid it may mean that he finds it better to have the work of art, as a system in his mind, kept distinct from that system to which "I" is the key. The contents of these systems are in great part the same; but the work of art may have to exclude parts of the self.

Thus Flaubert, an advocate of impersonality, felt, apparently, that his personality as a whole was lawless, so that he could not make of it a continent and pleasing work of art. In order to suppress certain aspects of it, certain anarchic idiosyncrasies, he found it helpful to think of his work as not himself. He speaks of his method as a discipline; "The man is nothing, the work is everything." But George Sand was right in telling him that the man was felt in the work. And he was no better artist than Goethe, who speaks freely in the first person.

It is possibly true of French literature, art or society, as of their government, that its rather formal discipline reflects a sense of inner conflict. They may need it.

EVERY artist, personal or impersonal, must be objective; he must see his self, if he depicts it, from a common standpoint; otherwise he cannot communicate it. Good autobiographies are not "subjective," but works of continent art. It may seem that anyone shameless enough might have written Rousseau's Confessions, but in fact only an accomplished artist could have done it. They are sincere, no doubt, but the effects are as much calculated as in a novel.

There is also a self-revelation which is unconscious, not artistic, evident in the authors of diaries, like Marcus Aurelius and Pepys. This element, however, is always present; we always communicate more than we are aware of. The behavior of the literary self is much like ordinary manners, which may be unconsciously pleasing, as in some children, or deliberately and artistically so, as in those we call well-bred.

WHEN Goethe's autobiography appeared Stendhal ridiculed it, saying that it would be read by posterity to see that there was a man with so absurd an idea of his own importance as to tell in four volumes how he did his hair at twenty and that he had a great aunt called Anichen. But Goethe knew he *was* important—the world had told him so—and that if you write your life at all you must fill it with detail, like a novel. Stendhal, not the least of egotists, was probably a little jealous that another and not himself should put over this kind of thing.

CRITICS are sometimes curiously superficial regarding the self. I recall one who praises the modesty of Dante because he only once mentions his own name. As if there were a publication in all literature more saturated with the sense of self than the Divine Comedy!

WHITMAN is hardly an egotist at all, in the proper sense of the word. He does not differentiate and gloat over himself in distinction from other men, but proclaims an inclusive Ego which might as well be called God.

When I listen to Whitman I think, What power! He is all they say and more. But it is long before I care to listen to him again. I crave more precise, varied and discriminate matter.

Selves and Bodies

THE feeling that self-revelation in a book is indecent is not unlike the similar feeling regarding the nude in art. The onlooker fails to see that such a revelation, if honest and well done, implies a self-discipline, even a kind of purity, incompatible with the grossness he imputes. A good painter of the nude may be licentious, but not for that reason.

A SELF, like a body, is delightful and disgusting by turns; refractory in either case, so that we are constantly struggling to control it in the interest of the common life. This gives rise to a certain presumption against incontinent display. Conventions of decency in dress, like table manners, have a real function as social discipline of the physical impulses. No doubt we might go quite unclothed without harm, but only on condition that it was customary, and that the social discipline had been established in some other form. To express the self nakedly, that is without social control, is truly indecent.

There are no "naked savages"; they are clothed in conventions not apparent to us, but as exacting as ours.

SCULPTURE and painting and literature uncover the soul and the body, restoring the wholeness of life. The restraint of art takes the place of clothes: the animal is released from his cage to perform under discipline.

Struggle

WE require that a writer give us in his own person, and no matter what the subject, some sense of the struggle that life is. He must not be too much at ease in Zion. Dana, of Two Years Before the Mast, a book of conflict and hardihood, added to it later a chapter describing a second visit to the Pacific Coast. It is far inferior. He had in the meantime, evidently, ceased to be the much-enduring sailorboy in whom we were proud to live, and become some sort of a philistine, a lawyer I believe—quite disgusting.

We like ease in a book, but only such as has been won by struggle. We should not care for the cathedral if we did not sense the quarry behind it.

PASSIVE meditation is a guide when it follows action: alone it moves in futile circles. Productive thought is a strenuous and costly function. It springs from struggle and is commonly instigated by a purpose, which, however, may be the purpose to build scientific or artistic truth. The fragmentary thinkers are no exception. Emerson and Montaigne were striving men who would not have had those thoughts without the purpose to utter them.

DO not the most moving of Shakspeare's Sonnets appear to record the appeasement of some inward struggle?* In Charles Lamb the gaiety would have but little zest without that background we know it had. Dante imparts not only figures of righteousness and beauty, but an arduous soul questing these things. Even Goethe is felt to be contending, though majestically. There may be exceptions, like Addison or Irving, but are they not, for this reason, somewhat wearisome?

A MAN may write on Love and Art and Peace and what not, but he will write to little purpose unless he has, back of it all, a natural ferocity.

WHEN one ceases from conflict, whether because he has won, because he has lost, or because he cares no more for the game, the virtue passes out of him.

Tranquillity

IN all epochs one who would write something tranquil and considerate must resist the spirit of the time, since, whatever the spirit of the time may be, it is never that.

Jealousy

ISAAC DISRAELI, in The Literary Character, has a chapter on the jealousy of writers, in which he gives instances of the unwillingness to confess obligation, as of Aristotle to Plato.

* E. g. NOB. 29, 33, 36, 40, 42, 61, 87, 129, 144, 147.

This is very general, but it is not altogether jealousy. For one thing, these obligations are often unconscious, to be discerned only in the future: it is our differences from our forerunners and associates of which we are most aware. Again, a man needs to see his own individuality in a sort of artistic completeness and detachment; he cannot realize and express himself otherwise; it is a matter of self-preservation.

Even Darwin, as all know who have read Samuel Butler's works on evolution, gave an inadequate account of his debt to his predecessors, certainly not from jealousy.

A young man, especially, may well leave to critics the task of discovering and defining his indebtedness to others. For him to attempt it would be an untimely anatomy, a partial suicide.

Criticism

NOTHING is more inciting than the literature of criticism. It appears that outside in the world there are people with leisure and inclination to ponder what has been written down, and to discover any secret there may be in it. You see that whatever you put into your work, even your very soul, can be read there by the initiated, and will be if it is worth reading.

IT is true that we have no absolute standards in criticism, any more than in morals, but in the one case as in the other a gifted and trained conscience may arrive at judgments which express the lasting, rather than the transitory, in human nature. Such judgments, when confirmed by diverse epochs and cultures, are perhaps as near the absolute as we need to get.

GOOD writers are never isolated, but always see their work in connection with that of others in the general organism of thought. Without this they could form no standard, no idea of their own function. Whitman was quite aware of the relation of his "yawp" to Emerson, Tennyson and other predecessors.

SAINTE-BEUVE is the most personal and whole-hearted of critics. His delight is to live himself into his subjects, recurring to a larger view for judgment. He puts sustained passion into it. He is not infallible, I presume, but who cares?

He is a sociologist in that he observes the individual and the social current with equal insight and minuteness, seeing the literary life as a variegated human whole continuous through time and space.

SAMUEL BUTLER (my contemporary), in his engaging Note-Books, rejects Goethe, Dante, Bacon and others of hardly less fame. This I take to be a kind of bravado that suits Butler well enough, and we may let it go at that. In general, as in this case, a failure to see merit in long-accepted authors throws more light on the critic than on the authors. There are always substantial grounds for these reputations—one school of critics may be fooled, but not several, from different times and cultures—and if a man does not feel them it means either that his mind is limited or that he has not taken the trouble to bring it into real contact.

A CREATIVE mind is rarely a good critic, because it sees everything with a view to its own uses, not by any general scale. Goethe is an exception, apparently because his creative impulse was so universal as not to involve a bias. And even he failed in judging social movements.

THE maxim of Fuller that "Learning hath gained most by those books by which the printer hath lost" is by no means invariably true, yet suggests a principle that applies as well now as ever. Works so original that there is no preparation for them cannot be popular. In spite of the alleged overestimate by Americans of their own authors, our greatest had no general welcome.

Original books that function in an established tradition are intelligently appraised by good critics, though they are rarely popular. But in the case of wide departure from tradition naïve human nature sometimes judges better than any critic. I mean that, like Burns's poems or Pilgrim's Progress, they may make their way first among unsophisticated people.

ONE who approaches a book, or any work of art, with the purpose of judging it, is hardly in a way to judge it well. That calls for a more relaxed and natural acquaintance. Read or lay it aside as you feel inclined; let its influence mature. Then, after months or years, observe how you feel about it, what life and growth it has taken on in your mind. The test of the good is that it stands being lived with, and this cannot be applied in a moment. Time and change are parties to all lasting judgments. Let us be grateful to honest critics, but not rely much upon them.

Self-Criticism

IN one sense we are our own best critics, in another quite incompetent. I can judge, better than anyone, whether I am doing good work according to my kind, but others must determine what my kind is worth. Let the robin build her own nest, after the manner of robins, and leave others to say how it compares with the oriole's nest or the mourning-dove's nest.

Is this that innermost and perfected thought which you would set afloat to be your self where you have no other?

"KNOW THYSELF" is very well, but let us remember that we can know ourselves only so far as we know others. A great use of study is to see our own thoughts by contrast, and so to become aware of them and to form some notion of their value. Too little reading is as fatal to individuality as too much. America, especially, is full of vigorous minds which remain futile for want of culture. As a trained singer can tell when his voice is in tune, though he cannot hear it as others do, so a cultured man, though he cannot evaluate his work, should know whether it has pertinence and function.

ONE should conceive that judgment on his book is to be passed by a conclave of wise and quiet spirits. They will take plenty of time, they will see through everything and consider the man behind it. They will not require infallibility, will not rebuke enthusiasm, will value hope. But they will dislike pretension, and if they find insincerity will read no farther.

LOWELL was perhaps the ablest critic within reach, but what he would have done to Thoreau's Week on the Concord and Merrimack Rivers, had it been submitted to him, we may guess from his review of it. One's own may be a poor thing, but it is all he has, and who else can be trusted to perceive and cherish it? It is a still small voice best heard in solitude.

AN author writes "My opinion of my own works would startle the world." Hardly. No conceivable extreme of arrogance or humility would startle anyone familiar with the self-estimates of artists.

ONE should never criticise his own work except in a fresh and hopeful mood. The self-criticism of a tired mind is suicide.

ON rereading parts of my first book, eighteen years old, I perceive none of that mental stress which it cost me in the writing. The excess of feeling that it seemed to have when I sent it to the publisher was all "subjective," embers of the productive fire now quite turned to ashes. There is a sort of rainbow fringe of emotion about our own recent work, for which we must, so far as possible, allow.

WHEN one is trying to write a book most of the work is done not in the actual writing, but in the unconscious processes, which move obscurely by day and night. It is interference with these, through a sort of subterranean competition, not mere loss of time, that makes other responsibilities detrimental.

IF you work slowly (but with ardor) you may educate yourself as you go. Almost by chance you do something better: you reflect upon it, see why it is better and make that the test of previous work, much of which you will now throw away.

THE way to know whether one has done his best is to let the work rest for some weeks. The restored mind will usually be unsatisfied and make new demands. And so again and again, indefinitely. The time will come, however, when the thing will seem to live and move with one's own life, to be mature and ready to be born. This indicates not that the work is really good, but that it is the best you can do until you get a better standard.

By putting aside his work and returning to it again and again, after long intervals and in other moods, a writer can, in some measure, anticipate the selection and concentration of time. In an epoch like ours we have to seek by individual continence that ripeness which the age lacks.

Hasty work is almost necessarily dishonest. It is necessarily bad: but to admit that it is bad is to throw up your hand. You must, then, conceal the truth, you must bluff, you must lie. Moreover you lose the greatest pleasure which writing affords, that of leisurely realization of one's ideal.

WHEN a thought arises freely, from the overflow of life in us, it shares our whole being, and its expression is not merely intellectual but total, joyous, poetic. This is the true juice, and it is poor stuff you get by squeezing.

Better an hour of inaction and one of good work than two of poor work, and so of days and months.

IT is good practice to copy one's own manuscript for the publisher, and to do it at leisure and with all one's wits about him. It compels a scrutiny not otherwise possible, and one is sure to make small changes, which may be peculiarly expressive.

One may become so familiar with an idea that he can no longer express it with spirit. He should write while it still has surprise for him, while he is a little in love with it.

Good writing is perhaps a finer art than speech, because of the deliberate and repeated attention it may expect, but it gets its vitality by suggesting speech, and always owes that a certain allegiance. There is no better test for the commoner faults of style than to read the thing aloud.

I work most effectively for a vague and remote public. Immediate publicity, or the prospect of it, is an unneeded and disquieting stimulant.

Getting free of a book to which you have bent your will for years is a task like throwing off the drink habit. Indeed the only way for a confirmed writer to get rid of an old book is to plan a new one.

It has been said that my social writings are deficient in censure. This may well be: I aim to think clearly and without bias, and find that I cannot do so if I mix thought with resentment. Possibly others will supply the censure.

Residual Satisfactions

The satisfactions which a faithful writer may be fairly sure of are at least two. First, that of living with and perfecting ideas, of high intercourse and endeavor. Second, an enlarging participation in the great life of which literature is the channel. You may read good books all your life and gain less insight into them than by a year or two of trying to produce one of your own.

There is no sweeter fruit of striving than to admire intelligently, to see how good a thing is and to know certainly you could never do it yourself. I once thought I could do literally anything, if I put my mind to it.

My book may or may not delight coming generations, it certainly gives me something cheerful to muse over from about four o'clock in the morning, when I wake up, until breakfast time.

Magazines

I hate "articles," and the few I have written were incidental to something else. What I like to do, and have done for the most part, is to delimit some large subject and brood over it as a whole, and for years, writing out paragraphs as they come to me, sitting down after breakfast to store the harvest of a wakeful night.

I prefer almost any tolerable book to the fragmentary matter in the magazines. That does not satisfy me, partly because it seems a little unreal or perfunctory, the authors not quite themselves but constrained by the "personality" of the magazine, and partly because I do not get it in large and quiet wholes. I meet a dozen people, as at a party, but do not get to know any of them.

The magazines foster competent writers, disciplined according to the standards of the day, but can hardly be propitious to indocile individuality. If one believes he is capable of something important he will do well not to think too much of them. A magazine is an institution, to whose system one must submit in order to be accepted. Knowing this he cannot write in a wholly free spirit. It welcomes individuality, but only within limits set by the prevailing taste. Hence work of a large and original kind has rarely appeared in magazines—not, for example, the most characteristic work of Emerson, Hawthorne, Thoreau, Mark Twain or Whitman; nor yet of Robert Frost and other notable contemporaries. Moreover the periodical compels you to be desultory: it is a house already framed to which you are permitted to add a detail, not a construction of your own.

A magazine must sell its wares immediately or not at all: a book can wait. It may even be published without regard to pecuniary return, as the best books (as well as the worst) often are.

The smaller the bits in which one publishes the more he exposes himself to be dissolved in the surrounding medium. In a larger whole he is more likely to preserve his real self.

I TAKE the——, thought to be the best of the literary monthlies. It is admirable; and yet at times I peculiarly detest it for a sort of pose which I seem to feel in it, and for a certain proprietary attitude towards the authors. The latter seem too docile, too conscientiously urbane. Urbanity is a good thing, but it ought to be spontaneous, and if so you may expect occasional lapses, especially when one is more concerned about the truth than about the impression he is making. I miss what I have heard called you-be-damnedness. I would give volumes of this publication for a thin book by Robert Frost.

Goethe

RESERVED writers may delight and enlarge us, but it takes the egotists to awaken an active self; Dante rather than Virgil, Montaigne or Emerson rather than Plato, Goethe, perhaps, rather than Shakspeare.

I feel in Goethe a distinctive self, working for personal and social ends; he has a will to influence, as well as reflect, the course of life. Because he was interested in the processes of his own growth he awakens a similar interest in me. The self of Shakspeare escapes me; or if I seem to feel it, in the Sonnets perhaps, I feel no social attitude. He is a greater poet, if you please, nobler, sweeter, more creative; but not, in this way, so helpful a man.

Goethe speaks often of the literary advantage to be had from contemplating pictures and sculpture. He kept casts from the antique by him for this purpose. "These noble forms," he says, "were a kind of secret antidote whenever the weak, the false, the mannered, threatened to win upon me."

It is indeed a certain atmosphere of art, of freedom, harmony and sane pleasure in life that gives Goethe such power to calm and cheer. I love to go with him: he gives me large, quiet thoughts. There is an assured joy in him, like that of a sunny landscape; he suggests agreeable plans. Other books seem thin compared with his. It is good to get into his great hospitable mind, where the truth is not cold or controversial, but calm, warm and mellow.

No books of thought are more friendly than the autobiographic writings of Goethe: they are wise, animated, human. They have, too, a great sweep and outlook, as if you were making a voyage around the world. His talk in his old age, as reported by Eckermann, is serene, hopeful, large-minded, full of matter. It has a good taste like plain bread. You get his universal curiosity and unfailing zeal, his sympathy with new movements, his faith.

One may learn from him to live well within one's powers, without anxiousness, and by intrinsic tendencies rather than opinion. So one may hope to be at home with himself, to have some measure of assurance, self-knowledge, wholeness of character, power without effort—to make his life a work of art.

I find Goethe above all wholesome. He looked as closely and kindly at the rocks as a mineralogist; and so with timber, the growth of plants, the human skeleton, human nature, social customs, architecture, painting, modeling, poetry, and the process of mankind in history. All he knew he knew by touch: there is no verbiage in him: he is a realist in whom, finally, there is a sense of God that is as real as all the rest.

Dante

THERE is a life in works of mediaeval architecture that comes from the spontaneity and individuality of each part. We find much the same in

Dante, whose rigid scheme is the container for spontaneous passages, each one, apparently, written for itself. He boasted, indeed, that he wrote from more direct inspiration than other poets:

"I am one who, when love inspires, record. . . ."*

It does not matter much that I only half understand Dante, that his background, his people, even his language, are dim. The first line brings back his spirit to me. I am aware of pride and beauty, of precise and tender vision, of a vast and right-demanding mind; I perceive again the grandeur of life.

He loved analysis, distinctions, precision. He was a professor of letters, a statesman; could easily have been a lawyer, have practised, perhaps, any learned profession of his day. This spirit of detail is related to his moral ardor. He does not find it all good, like Whitman, but is a hater.

Dante brought all life, in its essentials as they appeared to his time, within a work of art. He also saw and judged it, in large and in detail, as a moral whole. There is in him a grandeur of synthesis; of knowledge, beauty and righteous passion; that is found nowhere else. Who can think on Dante and not believe in God?

Pascal

INSTITUTIONAL writers die with their institutions. I cannot read those Jansenist arguments upon which Pascal put most of his work; his casual thoughts live because they speak for human nature. "When we do not know the truth of a matter," he says, "it is well that there should be a common error to fix the spirits of men." What a light is that, on the church, on all institutions!

Think of his saying that all the unhappiness of men comes from one thing, that is, from not knowing how to live at peace in a room! His idea is that life is so bad that anything is better than to sit still and think about it: hence our busyness. That there can be any positive good in activity seems not to occur to him.

I find in Pascal a passionate and searching spirit, wise in a strenuous way but not genial, with much wit and no humor, and more pity than fellowship. His thoughts do not, as in Montaigne, flow comfortably from a homely way of life; you feel no such quiet background, but a spirit

* Purg., xxiv.

of controversy, rather, and a more conscious rhetoric. Although his teaching is one of extreme abnegation he is not to be counted among the humble spirits like Thomas à Kempis. Indeed I know no writer who has more of a delicate intellectual pride.

His rhetoric is fascinating: compression is carried to a point where you share the tension that impelled him to it. He is high, clear and disdainful, like Dante. But of no such sustained flight. Failing health, following on a precocious development and his heroic struggle with the Jesuits, drove him, apparently, to morbid ascetism, a shrinking view of the world, and death at thirty-nine years.

Bacon

BACON'S ESSAYS are matter from his note-book, revolved, compressed and illustrated. He thought "I will write what is true for all time" and speaks of current events with detachment, as if from the point of view of posterity. He loves good images and hates excess. There is a certain freedom and grandeur of perception in him. His comparison of Fortune to the Milky Way is in this large style: "The way of Fortune is like the Milken Way in the sky: which is a meeting or knot of a number of small stars, not seen asunder but giving light together. So there are a number of little and scarce discerned virtues, or rather faculties and customs, that make a man fortunate."

He is worldly, an opportunist in morals, more pleasing to a disillusioned middle age than to youth. You do not feel, as you do in Emerson or Montaigne, that he saw himself in any clear and noble light. He does not exercise the immediate moral ascendency of those others. Largely concerned with public affairs there is a zest in his treatment of such themes as Empire, or Seditions and Troubles, that shows he was indeed fit for high counsel. The English aristocracy, a race of politicians and administrators, has made his fame.

If he had a fourth of Montaigne's geniality he would be four times as much read.

Montesquieu and de Tocqueville

MONTESQUIEU does not disguise the fact that his Esprit des Lois is made up of imperfectly unified reflections. He does not subordinate himself to a plan, but is personally there in every paragraph. De Tocqueville is more systematic, more speculative, not so pithy, not so hard-headed, not so great.

La Bruyère

La Bruyère strikes one as a naturally timid man who has somewhat desperately made up his mind to utter his whole self, come what may. He is conscious of his egotism and takes a fearful joy in it. He is so evidently a sensitive man writing from his sensibilities that we keep asking ourselves "What happened to him to make him say that?" And yet, although he often speaks in the first person, he is never relaxed and familiar like Montaigne, but always strenuously an artist.

He is animated, specific, penetrating: you get the sense of eager speech. Writing under a vivid impression he revised only enough to clarify that impression. He has humorous exaggerations, like an American: "L'on marche sur les mauvais plaisants, et il pleut par tous les pays de cette sort d'insectes"; as we might say "The woods are full of silly jokers." It is not judicial, long-pondered truth, as in Bacon, nor secluded, self-disciplinary meditation, as in Marcus Aurelius, nor yet a laconic and luminous science of human nature, as in la Rochefoucauld: it is just a vivid commentary on life.

The interest is largely in watching for the *tours,* those cutting turns of phrase which he rarely fails to bring off. How will he do it this time?

There is so much of his wit, and so even in quality, that one remains with an impression of meritorious industry.

Samuel Butler

There is something sociable in language itself, the common medium of human solidarity, so that perhaps no thinker, not even Marcus Aurelius, has written his thoughts without some vague sense of appealing to his fellows. And there are all degrees of this, from the solitude of Marcus to that self-conscious performance before an audience which most writing is. Somewhere on this scale, not far from the beginning, there is an attitude which is primarily reflective and self-pleasing, but also has something distinctly genial, as of one who is accustomed to a kindly circle, though it does not happen to be about him at the moment. I find this in Samuel Butler, among others, who for all his cynical views of the family is a gentle and friendly person, as well as ingenious, humorous and wise.

I care less for his famous books, Erewhon and The Way of All Flesh, than for his desultory Note-Books. These are more natural, and you can find in them something for almost any mood. The Authoress of the Odyssey is a joy, and his Alps and Sanctuaries the sort of travel book of which there are not nearly enough.

His humor is bound up with his command of certain original points of view, especially as to evolution, which he had won by shrewd observation and severe thinking. Between these and everyday life it plays, illuminating both—as when he says "The hen is an egg's way of producing another egg."

Being recent his fame is unsettled. The question is, Has he or has he not something genial and unique that people will come again and again to taste?

Quiet in Books

THE feeling some books give of silence, as if, on a still night, one listened to the water dripping in the gutters, comes perhaps from the sense that they are solitary meditations, not communications *to* any one, which would suggest sound. They seem to be without a human audience, written, as it were, to God; so that you rise with the author out of all compliances. The pen, like Dante's, points straight to the Dictator. An inner passion for truth, not requiring immediate appreciation, gives the writer assurance and universality. I find this in Marcus, in some of the Psalms, in Thomas à Kempis in George Herbert, in a few of Shakspeare's Sonnets, in the best of Emerson and much of Thoreau.

Perfect meditation has a character and beauty of its own. It is a mature and spontaneous utterance falling like ripe leaves on a still day in the fall of the year. The reader may watch it if he pleases, it exists for itself, not for him. The thoughts of solitude are heard in solitude, and have an inward chime that public thoughts must lack.

Would it not be well to copy one's manuscript on still summer mornings in a remote place, and hush all the noise out of it?

VERBAL cleverness commonly lowers the tone of meditation: one does not address God in that way. Yet in George Herbert's devout poems there are anagrams and sportive imagery that do not seem out of place. *He* can do it.

Thoreau

A BOOK of meditations should be a place in which the writer lives quite at ease, saying familiarly what he thinks, with only friends about him. It may have a hearth-thought, a kind of fire-place for all the family of impressions to gather about and keep warm. Thoreau says, profoundly I think, "Homeliness is almost as great a merit in a book as in a house, if the reader would abide there."* And again, "A book should be so true as to be intimate and familiar to all men as the sun to their faces,—such a word as is occasionally uttered to a companion in the woods in summer, and both are silent."†

Thoreau was tense, proud and quickly perturbed by contact with other persons. He found release and sanity in nature, ascetic living and classic reading; while the planning and composition of his books afforded him self-expression and hope. Although a disciple of Emerson he was only superficially like him, indeed not much like any other writer.

It seems to me that Emerson does not hold the reader by his mere personality and style, as Thoreau does, but that we require him to be saying something profound or uplifting. Their attitudes are very unlike; one is a prophet uttering his inspirations before an audience, the other a meditative thinker hardly conscious of a public.

Henry James says of Thoreau, in his Hawthorne, that he was worse than provincial, he was parochial. But is it so certain which is parish and which capital? With whom does one feel in a larger place, with Henry James or with Thoreau?

He is less hortatory than Emerson; he fortifies our self-trust rather by example than precept, letting fall his philosophy in the form of articulate meditations that we may take or leave as we see fit. His sentences are as natural, secluded and refreshing as the woodland springs he loved to frequent. So soon as I begin to read him I feel reassured regarding the things that appear true to me alone, and ashamed of my doubts and conformities.

No one has deeper wisdom for the use of a writer. "Report a life," he says, "do not exhibit a talent." "The scholar may be sure that he writes the tougher truth for the calluses on his palms. They give firmness to the sentence. . . . A sentence should read as if its author, had he held a plow instead of a pen, could have drawn a furrow deep and straight to the end." "Yet, after all," he adds, "the truly efficient laborer will not crowd the day with work . . . he is anxious only about the fruitful kernels of time. Though the hen should sit all day she could lay only one egg, and besides, would not have picked up materials for another."*

* A Week etc. 111 (Walden Edition).

† Journal, I, 282.

* A Week etc., 109, 110.

A book like his Walden has something infinite about it. It is not the outcome of any one impulse or point of view, but is a whole man, and whenever I read a page with care I discover something I had not found before. His prose, at its best, is passionate, musical, still, an inward voice, and strains of it linger in the memory.

I have found no reading more salutary to a weary mind than Thoreau's Journal—in fourteen volumes. It imparts assurance and a sober joy in life, while the images it calls up are of out-of-door things wholesome to think of. This work has also the advantage of being so long, and so easily forgotten as to its details, that when you reach the end you can begin again and scarcely notice the repetition.

Thomas à Kempis

It takes small Latin to read Thomas, whose words are simple and their syntax plain. His De Imitatione Christi is a book which, with almost no anecdote or imagery, is yet of the most vivid reality, that of deep and quiet feeling. Like many great books it is narrow in range; its charm is that of a few high and appeasing thoughts repeated in a thousand passages, each with a life and spontaneity of its own. It has the form of solitary meditations, and was no doubt based on such, but it seems too finished to be less than a work of art, prepared, probably, for the use of the younger brethren of the order to which he belonged.

As compared with Marcus Aurelius, Thomas is less strenuous and happier. He has that joy in the inner life which is so attractive in the Christian tradition, the same that finds expression in the poems of St. Francis and of George Herbert. "Spiritual consolations," he says, "surpass all the delights of the world and the pleasures of the flesh." Compared with Emerson he is less stimulating, less intellectual; and if one seeks composure rather than incitement he may be a more congenial companion.

We must not forget, however, in the interest of such comparisons, that Thomas himself says we are not to dispute concerning the virtues of the saints, each of whom served God in his own way and is not to be judged greater or less than another.

Part Three

Thinking

Originality

DISCOVERIES in thought are much like those in geography, the first condition is the enterprise and persistence that gets you into unexplored regions. If you can gain a fresh point of view the rest is easy.

THERE would be plenty of original men if intellectual brilliancy sufficed. The real sifter is the dogged endurance required to work to exhaustion day after day, finding oneself at the close strained, nervous, unfit for anything else, and with nothing surely accomplished—going on thus for months and years. Not that there is any uncommon hardship in this, but few will undergo it voluntarily for a dubious end. It implies a need, a passion, one *cannot* let go.

The born thinker is excited by the prospect of truth, by the hope of going deeper, of seeing things more nearly as they are than has been done before. He will lie awake nights, he will batter against the impossible until he is desperate and almost suicidal. There is a factor of temperament in it: you must not only have a good brain but it must be set to go off at the right touch and no other.

TWO things are notably useful in opening up fresh views; a precise and thoughtful record of the facts one sees for himself, and a persistent endeavor to see all around one's ideas, to assimilate them with fact from every standpoint, so that nothing of their meaning may escape.

ALL growth is by the working out of vague impulse which, struggling with actuality, is defined, adapted, developed and merged with the actual in a new whole. So man himself begins in vague potentiality, grows by struggle while the impulse lasts, slows up, crystallizes and dies.

It is thus with original thought; the clear things are those already worked out.

The student reads finished books and so lives in what is organized rather than inchoate. They state the obvious problems and appear to solve them. His only escape is to look long and hard at the facts as he finds them, make his own problems and search for the answers.

ORIGINALITY begins in our reaction to the necessary events of life, to things that come up hard against us. We are apt to neglect these and clog our minds with ideas from without that have no direct and functional relation to us. Few students understand that reading is the food, not the germ, of good thinking, and nourishes us only in so far as we can assimilate it to our own unique organism. They look to reading for their problems, instead of for light on problems they already have. If you are destined to do anything original there is some germ of it growing in you now, and your first need is to discover and cherish that.

I HAVE heard a student censured for working out his own idea before learning all that others had done on the subject. But he was right; one may know too much, especially at first. The time for exhaustive reading is when you have worked out your own ideas with some fulness and in a spirit of discovery. Having thus nursed your offspring beyond the period of infant mortality you may let him prove and mature himself in the stream of life. Now is the time for deliberation, for comparison, for ascertaining what real contribution, if any, you have to offer, and for bringing it to perfection.

No doubt it is hard, at this stage, to contain and mature your idea instead of publishing it, but if you have not the restraining conscience of the artist you will do nothing worth noticing in any case.

ORIGINALITY wells out from sources subconscious and somewhat mysterious. You must let the subterranean waters accumulate. A too strenuous life will dry them up. When "the river of God is full of water" we may hope for inspiration.

AN original man is apt to say and do naïve things, because, in fact, he *is* naïve, arrives at his views rather by the direct use of experience than by way of the ideas of other men. Give him time and he will consider also what others have found and omit that part of his naïvety which, in a large view, has no value.

The ambition to appear sophisticated, or, what amounts to the same, the fear of appearing naïve, is a fence to keep us within the commonplace. Indeed nothing is more sterile than sophistication, which usually consists in knowing too much about inessential and transitory matters.

THERE are many large thinkers and many keen observers of detail, but few who are both. The habit of seeing facts freshly and also in relation to principles is the great and difficult thing.

TO observe well takes great energy, more than the hardest reading. One must cast off habit and see as if for the first time, as a child. He must, as it were, be born again.

I WOULD aim at verity, spontaneity, thoroughness, rather than originality. The last comes, in my observation, by working out simple ideas with more completeness and naïvety than others do. Nor is it good to compare your thoughts frequently with those of other people, asking "Am I original?" Follow them to the end, in the spirit of truth, and then see if they are worth anything.

If a man will take his place before almost any fact and scrouge down into it, he will come upon something not adequately known.

THE question of credit for originality had better be left to historians. The desire for it is natural, but a man cannot judge his own case, nor that of his rivals, and appears fatuous when he assumes to do so.

The great and arduous thing is to contribute something. Let a man read all he finds helpful, acknowledge any debt he is aware of, keep to himself any estimate he may form of his own importance, and not worry as to whether he has or has not repeated something that Vico said in the eighteenth century.

System and Spontaneity

To think well one must know how to reconcile system with spontaneity. It is easy to think when the event suggests and the mood inclines; hateful to force a reluctant brain over a prescribed road. And yet a constructive mind cannot be fully aroused by desultory thought; it must feel itself working on a whole. You must manage to have a plan and mostly to forget it.

GOETHE offers an example of the union of freedom with structure. He worked *stellenweise*—passage-wise—as he says, at whatever happened to interest him, but by brooding over his subjects they took on a natural system in his mind. He had always under way a variety of projects which gave function to observations otherwise desultory. His books are written in contempt of formal order, but have the vaguely organic process of nature herself.

BOOKS which require you to carry a system in your head are hard reading and seldom worth the trouble. An enduring philosophy must appeal to every-day, human modes of thinking. How many systematic works are read after a hundred years? Very few, and most of those not very systematic. The disconnectedness of Plato, Montaigne, Pascal and Emerson is a main reason for their acceptance.

IF a man has a system it is injudicious to keep reminding us of the fact; better insinuate it in a diet of agreeable details. He himself may well beware of it lest he write merely to fill it out. I find my own system tiresome to think of, except at rare intervals, and no doubt others will find it more so. We love truth best when it makes us free. A serious work should have a natural structure which the reader can discover if and when he pleases. It is good to display a subject with unity enough to make it intelligible, and yet not without an alluring unfinality.

How to Grow Ideas

THE labor of thinking is like that of one striving to produce a new variety of fruit. He has thousands of seeds at hand (namely his notes), any one of which may develop into something rare. He goes tediously over these, selects the more promising, and starts them growing. When they have sprouted he goes over them again, weeding out all but a few. From the best of these he gets new seed. And if, by continuous selection, any good varieties are produced, he propagates these largely and gives them the best soil and culture.

WHEN one has achieved the first draft of a work and sees and feels the whole, is a great time. The view excites him; he can hardly think of anything else; he seems just about to pluck the longed-for fruit. Ideas come fast, problems clear up, the whole engenders the parts. It is now that by intimate touches he can put himself into his work, can attain, perhaps, a real superiority. Now is the time to go slowly; it would be sad to slip on the last round of the ladder.

A LIVING organism of thought makes its own choices. When you have got so far you will no longer be in doubt as to what belongs to your work: it knows its own like a mother.

A SOUND mind is an organic human whole, and may do better work in each of several provinces than if it is narrowed to one. The mere attempt to do something liberal and different may make one a better specialist, as Goethe's essays in painting and sculpture made him a better writer.

AS one grows older he sees more clearly the sequent, in some sense inevitable, character of his mental history. He can perhaps trace a strenuous mind in his ancestry. From infancy his thought, endlessly revolving, has worked itself out into organic wholes of which he was himself, perhaps, unaware. The idea that seems new to-day you find in last year's notes. All is growth.

Are we not all subject to a cycle of recurring interests, or rather to many cycles, of longer and shorter periods, like the swells of the sea and the waves and wavelets thereon? Perhaps once in six months one has a spell of brooding over pictures, another of reading books of travel, etc., etc.

Dried Truth

AFTER all, we relish abstract truth; there are uses for a dried and labeled idea that it did not have in life—"clean and dry as fossil truth" says Thoreau. We treasure the formulations of La Rochefoucauld although most of his ideas are rather matters of course in novels. His saying, "Hypocrisy is the homage that vice pays to virtue" is immortal as a statement, but must always have been rather obvious as a fact. Boileau justly remarked that the mind of man teems with confused ideas and vague half glimpses of the truth, and that we like nothing better than to have one of these well elucidated and clearly presented. Perhaps, as the names suggest, this is especially a French taste.

EPIGRAMMATIC philosophy may interpret common experience: it cannot deal with questions which must be approached, like the higher peaks of the Himalayas, only after systematic preparation. If it is everybody's problem you may treat it in this way; if for experts, no.

Motives

I FEEL little interest in any thinking that has a merely practical reference; my mind will not work with zest unless it feels itself free and, as it were, in a serene and immortal light.

Yet the life of every man, as of every age, is a struggle to bring order and joy out of his experience, and the memorable thought is the one that helps in this struggle.

ONE does not think alone. If he cherishes solitary thoughts it is with some sense of realizing and asserting these in the world. He builds himself for the whole.

I HAVE no sustained philanthropy, and feel weak or slightly hypocritical when I find myself urging reforms. What is real to me is the perception and expression of lasting truth about human life. In this I delight for its own sake, like any scholar or artist. The hope of it keeps me going.

Milieu

IT was a rule of Descartes "never to receive anything as true which I do not know clearly *(evidemment)* to be so, that is to avoid carefully haste and prejudice, and not to include more in my judgments than what presents itself so clearly and distinctly to my mind that I have no occasion to doubt it."

This is no safeguard against illusion. The ideas we get by suggestion from the crowd, or from the universal opinion of the hour, have precisely this distinctness, and as they come unconsciously we are unaware of haste or prejudice.

A universal prejudice we cannot escape, although those of our class or nation may be combated by wider contacts.

I do not know that there is any one principle more essential to the understanding of human life than this: that the premises of our thought, the things that appear to us matters of course, so that to question them is merely ridiculous, are just those things which we believe only because we are used to them, and have no other foundation whatever.

Controversy

LET our struggle be with the facts, with life, rather than with other writers. We cannot have the spirit of truth and the spirit of controversy at the same time.

ONE who writes controversy digs his own grave. Only serene thoughts will last.

THERE is always a controversy. If your writings are part of it they attract more attention from contemporaries, perhaps, because of interest in the game, but have less chance with posterity, because controversies are ephemeral. Emerson's indifference to the disputes of technical philosophers has caused him to be neglected by that class, but is one of the traits that have raised him to a class above them.

ALL or nearly all the books on social questions which have a large immediate circulation owe their vogue to a partisan element. They appeal to property-holders, to under dogs, to the impecunious intelligentsia, to the sexually repressed, to Nordics, Negroes, Fundamentalists. Their fitness is to an emotional rather than to a scientific interest. Books written for the latter must be content with a small though possibly lasting acceptance.

Z HAS written a good book, laborious, penetrative, illuminating. He has prefixed to it an introductory chapter in which he says, in effect, that his method is the only sound one, and that the point of view of another group of students is absurd—in short announces himself, quite gratuitously, as a very circumscribed man.

IT is creditable to have an original idea, but to have one and not bore people with it is distinguished. Why spoil the impression by urgency? How grateful is the light touch, how pleasing one who appears to care more for truth and beauty than for his own claim upon it!

I AM oppressed by any sense of controversy in what I write. In the hope of truth and pleasantness I find a more fruitful excitement.

The Subservience of Contradiction

A WRITER whose aim is to be unlike others is liable to a subservience of contradiction. That is, he after all gets his cue from them, takes the other end of the same rope. Originality raises new questions. It is the mark of a rarely stable mind that antagonism cannot drive it to extremes.

IN every time the conspicuous radicals are likely to be contradictors and hence subservient, while real changes gestate in obscurity.

CONTEMPORARY thought may be explained in no small degree by the subservience of contradiction. Much "scientific" animus—that is, materialistic and mechanistic—is in this way subservient to theology. Behaviorism reflects mysticism.

Some are so impressed by their emancipation from religious and social myths that they seem unable to get over it. They see everything from this standpoint, cannot take a fresh and natural view, go about exclaiming on all occasions "How we *were* fooled!"

WAS not Nietzsche too much of a controversialist to be a very great thinker—as distinguished, I mean, from a prophet or a poet? Was not his thought so much determined by antagonism to that of others that its interest, involved in a particular situation, is for a period rather than for humanity at large? His views on religion and the church seem to me of this sort, expressing reaction against Christianity rather than a composed and universal view. How much more potent is Goethe's criticism of the church, or Emerson's, mostly unconscious but implicit in their whole way of thinking, than the attacks of Nietzsche. He shows too much concern.

His incomprehension of democracy and feeling that "the herd" must have a master, reflects a mind which itself lacked poise and common sense. His interpretations of life are impassioned, subtle and grandiose, but flighty; not sure, serene and fit to anchor to.

I HAVE sometimes wondered whether competitive debating, with no aim at truth or cooperation, was not a mere vice. Does it not deform and abort the process of healthy discussion?

Notes from Practice

I HAVE found advantage in turning my mind loose on a question and writing at random, yet precisely, whatever thoughts came to me regarding it, no matter how trivial they might seem. Sometimes you will find yourself thinking with a strange freshness, as in dreams.

WHEN my children were small I used sometimes to sit near one of them with a note-book and set down everything he did—so far as I could—for a given time. It is a good plan in any study to observe for a while carefully but with no definite purpose. You are likely to see things you would otherwise overlook, and perhaps strike a new trail.

I DO not worry when I lose sight of a budding idea. I am sure to find it growing cheerfully next time I work in that corner of the garden. Any thought that you can lose is not truly yours.

But a certain ardor of expression should be caught on the fly: it does not always return.

THE thinker should "intend his mind," but not narrowly or at the cost of human living. He who would think for mankind must think as a man.

IN order to resume a work of thought it is often best not to pick up the stale fragments but to make a fresh start. Consider the general subject in some aspect that attracts you and write as the spirit moves; you can make the connections later.

WE rarely gain a higher or larger view except as it is forced upon us through struggles which we would have avoided if we could.

Children's Philosophy

ONE of the recollections of my early childhood—I was five or six years old—is the arrival at a kind of Berkeleyan idealism. I decided that we could never *know* anything, not even the swinging chain of the fence that separated my yard from that of the boy next door.

MARY (aged five years) says, "I don't cry any more when I go to bed. I lie down and I think and wonder and guess."

Part Four

Art, Science, And Sociology

Building

I AM building a boat, and many eager hours go into it. I am most myself when I am making something. Life needs no further justification, "for this the day was made." I see, feel and smell strips of wood, planes, nails and paint. I live in these things, planning and forming. I love to contrive, to overcome difficulties in fitting the boards, to improve my methods of planing. To construct, to create, with oak and cypress, clout nails and casing nails, to mould the materials to a new function, your own idea, using your mind some and your muscles more; this is what engages me so that I scarcely care to think of anything else. I have driven some three thousand nails into my boat, each put into a hole previously bored for it, and clinched, all requiring care. I notice that visitors view my work with a certain enthusiasm, as if it were the ideal occupation. Who would not wish to build a boat?

I LIKE to enter a planing-mill, discuss the making of my doors and window-frames with the foreman amid the screech of the saws and planers, figure out the prices and leave my order.

IT is pleasing to think that the men who built and carved the mediaeval churches were not unlike me, that I have some of their passion when I work at my oaken table. They had far more knowledge and training, were in a great current of such production; it was a social institution, their work was habitual, customary and profitable. But I have the same native feeling, and what in me, because of social conditions, is only incidental and abortive, might then have been a career.

ONE may get from handwork a sense of craftsmanship and of the fruits of patience that can be transferred to more abstract endeavors. An oak sideboard that took me two summers to make was (like Gibbon's service with the militia) not without advantage to my studies. Such work makes one familiar with processes every step of which must be considerately done in order to get a satisfying result. If you hurry you go wrong and cannot fail to see it.

The Glamour of Art

WHEN, a young man, I worked in the Census Bureau at Washington, I used to spend spare or stolen hours lounging in the Corcoran Gallery. My work was of a kind which did not restrict me very closely, and I was at liberty to occupy much of my time in any way that I deemed the good of my country required. At that date most of the pictures were in one vast room on the second floor. I remember that when I ascended the central stairway, and the expanse of serene and joyous form and color opened on my view, I felt an emotion that lifted me quite out of the tedium and worry of the Office. What a glamour the paintings have in memory! I recall one warm picture of the valley of the Adige that filled me with a joy I seldom if ever had from such a scene in nature.

And all my life I have found that regarding works of art and brooding over artists and their ways is not only delightful in itself but enlarges and renews my spirit and way of thinking. I hardly know why; it is partly the relief and release that comes from thinking of man as a maker of beauty, and of myself, even, as possibly a sharer in this. One gets a fresh sense of life.

THE practice of art, the very idea of it, is a sort of heaven for the hidden self. It means that what you got a secret and timid joy from can be unfolded, communicated, made the chief matter of life. What you cherished almost in shame has, it appears, an honorable function in the world of men.

I AM more in love with the idea of art than with any or all forms of it.

J. F. MILLET said, "The beautiful consists not so much in the thing represented as in the longing to represent it;" meaning, I suppose, that the spirit of the artist is the chief part of what is communicated and enjoyed. He communicates himself joying in these forms and colors. According to Fromentin (himself a painter) painting is an infallible witness of the moral state of the painter at the moment when he held the brush.

I am fond of writers, like Fromentin, who appreciate one art in terms which are applicable to others, and to life at large. Of Paul Potter he says, "More than any painter in this honest school he spoke of naïvety, of patience, of circumspection, of persevering love of truth. . . . All his originality comes to him from thence. His greatness also."*

I LIKE to think of myself obscurely working out honest details, as if with my carving chisels. It is a sweet, free, humble life, away from that hot breath of communicated passion that dries up delicate things.

ART promises that freedom of which we dream. It is a personal and creative treatment of life, at work primarily in the senses, and thence up through the imagination and the reason. It may be a child with his colors or a philosopher with his system. An artist *cannot* stop as others do when he has done as well as people expect.

To desire to be an artist is to desire to be a complete man in respect to some one function, to realize yourself utterly. A man is a poor thing who is content not to be an artist. An artist cannot fail; it is success to be one.

A LIVING art offers to the constructive spirit a tradition and a technique through which he may fulfill himself and merge in the achievement of mankind. By undergoing its discipline one earns the right and the power to dwell with and to bring forth a joyous self.

IT is a paradox of work in any art to call for unperturbed naturalness, and yet to require an intensity with which this is hardly compatible. It must report passion with equanimity.

ART smoothes the brow and rounds the eye, and we love artists because they transmute life into truth and joy. The very condition of perceiving art is a certain renewal of spirit. You aspire towards culture, read, study, listen to lectures; and nothing comes of it except a little pedantry. But meanwhile, if you have any spontaneity about you, it may happen that certain pictures, certain books, certain buildings, keep coming back to mind and awakening desire. You do not know why and it is better that you should not. The more you become like a little child the more hope there is of your discovering, at last, what art really is.

The Artist's Public

ONE does not become an artist without the sense of an audience, but he will do no excellent work until this sense becomes so generalized, so assimilated to himself, that he pays no regard to the immediate public.

* Maitres d'autrèfois, 120, 221.

THE artist may take no joy in the thought of popular success, but his aim is social, he loves to think that he has a hidden treasure to which he is adding day by day, that he is secretly enriching the common life of men.

AMONG the followers of any art there is a society, mostly second-rate, of the present place and hour, and a higher society of the masters of all time. The artist needs both, but only the latter can lift him above mediocrity.

An artist should see his work as nearly *sub specie aeternitatis* as he can. If he sees it by what his friends will think or the critics say he is lost.

THERE are three elements in art: creative joy, technique, and receptive joy; of which the first and the last are not separate, for the artist's joy is partly an anticipation of the joy he hopes to give, while the joy of the recipient is partly from sympathy with that of the artist.

A bit of carving in which the carver has pleased himself fixes your attention. You sympathize with the maker, his interest reaches you and you enjoy a vicarious self. In this appeal to creative impulse art has something that nature has not: we can hardly sympathize with God.

Heritage

IT is the nature of art to build languages, of which the verbal is but one. In sound, color, form and motion we beget evolving incarnations in which the human spirit can live and grow.

A PAINTER observes the light from a window falling pleasantly on the adjacent wall and table. It interests him because, as a painter, his being is bent upon the creation of such effects, he has been formed by a tradition and is the organ of a productive impulse in the human race. He sees not so much what is there as what he can make of it. His imagination and his practiced fingers start into action, and he makes a note which is one of many going to build up a whole he may already have in view. So, brooding, sketching, refining, feeling his way deeper and deeper into visual life, he at last produces a work colored through and through with a learned joy and fit to impart it to others. Less than nature in one sense in another it is far more, man has taken a hint and worked it out to issues of his own.

EVERY artist is in some degree a Way, a redeemer, a giver of new life. And a fine art is a continuing and perfected Way in which such life flows abundantly.

THE people who built the cathedrals were no more patient than you and I are, perhaps of no more ability, but they had an ideal that would not let them off with small things. This they owed to the times, to the conception of great and living architectural forms which had gradually been built up by the endeavors of preceding ages. Now the chain of practice is broken and the vision gone.

OUR minds not only rationalize but hedonize. They tend to work over their content until it is joyous as well as consistent. Thus we are likely to mould almost anything to beauty if we have time to cherish and brood over it. If we do not do so with our age it is because we are restless and unripe, not because the age is incapable of beauty. Its peculiar ugliness is no more hopeless than that of other ages.

THE notion that an untaught taste can judge of art has this grain of truth: there may be an openness to new beauty that the instructed taste has lost. But this openness can do nothing without culture. By culture I do not mean explicit knowledge, but that natural growth of appreciation which comes by attentive familiarity with the objects. People of a fine ear acquire an understanding of music rapidly and often without instruction, but it must be acquired. Taste always has a history, both in the individual and in social tradition.

EACH kind of art has a growth, and art as a whole puts forth new forms of beauty age by age, but it is not cumulative like science. Every perfect form is final in that way, and we cannot say that the later forms are superior to the earlier.

Criticism progresses, because knowledge is cumulative and criticism is partly knowledge. A man of fine sense born now can become larger and perhaps surer in his judgments than he could have been in any former epoch.

PRODUCTIVE spirits must do something different, must seek a distinctive self, and yet rarely have the power to strike out in an essentially new direction. So if the general movement of which they are a part is decadent they usually develop it in that sense. There is an organic growth which the individual can hardly escape.

Art and Conduct

ARTISTS may or may not be good men, but perhaps there is none who is not a better man than he would be without his art. In one province at least he undergoes the best sort of discipline, that which is self-imposed for love.

ONE might well aim to make his life before the world a work of art, only bearing in mind that it is not good art unless what the world does not see accords with what it does.

TOO much art, ready-made by others, is enervating. It is our function to create, not to luxuriate, "Art is not a pastime," said J. F. Millet, "it is a battle-field."

ROMAIN ROLLAND says, "The artist is the voice of the earth, and the one who binds together all the sons of the earth. A rich man cannot be a great artist." What of Rubens and Goethe? I take it that the case is difficult, as with the Kingdom of Heaven, but not impossible.

No doubt there is something in personal wealth repellent to the artistic sense; one feels that it is the exaggeration of a part, does not lie peacefully in the landscape. Simple things and ways bring all humanity into the picture. We feel this more than men did in the past because when social order was based in part on visible prestige and display, private luxury had a function which it has now lost.

A MAN seeks to control and harmonize his life so that he may be at peace. But nature, perhaps, is not ready to round off so small a piece of creation, and he finds himself swept into conflict by impulses that are part of some larger whole. There are greater issues than his comfort.

The beauty of life is a dynamic unfinished beauty, not a work of completed art: it is like that of a play whose outcome we cannot foresee. One who is quite at peace with himself may be said to be out of harmony with nature.

OUR individual lives cannot, generally, be works of art unless the social order is also.

I SEE few faces that express a clearly achieved character. Is our time a bad artist?

Or did the artist, and not life, give clearness to Holbein's faces?

A LITERARY artist is rarely an active social radical. He may see horrors, but he will either see them as conditions of beauty, (which is to justify them) or, being sensitive, he will shut them out and build some kind of a wall against them. He is very apt, however, by depicting an ideal life, to be a cause of radicalism in others, like Rousseau or Emerson. There is also one way in which an artist, as such, may be a reformer. He may turn his artistic sense upon the organic movement of society, see life as a play, and strive to fulfill the action; not hating the villain but requiring that he give way at the fitting time. Many social workers are, in fact, of a somewhat artistic type, not at all bitter against evil, but cheerfully convinced that it must go and pleased with their own role in speeding its departure.

An Art of Society?

If language is subject matter for art, and manners, why not the social order itself, of which these are aspects? Is not the creation of a fair society the supreme and inclusive art?

Our democracy might be a work of art, a joyous whole, rich in form and color, free but chastened, tumultuously harmonious, unfolding strange beauty year by year. Each of us would be spontaneously functional, like the detail in great architecture.

Art and Science

The idea of a gulf between art and science, as things different in kind, seems to be recent. Leonardo da Vinci, with his attainments in mathematics and physics, and being a great painter withal, reveals no sense of it, but looks upon all his studies as *scienze* or branches of knowledge. The basis for our view seems to be that the sciences are cumulative, an imperishable and ever-increasing structure, while the arts bloom and die like flowers. This notion perhaps arose as science was observed to develop a technique of its own, quite different from that of art.

It is a sound distinction, because practical, but not so sharp as is commonly supposed. In general our branches of study, judged by this test, are both sciences and arts, and the name you call them by will depend upon which aspect you consider more essential. There is a science of natural appearances and of technique connected with painting, but we regard this as subsidiary to the art; there is an art of description and of conjecture connected with geology, but we regard this as subsidiary to the science. The worker almost always practices both, and the worker in science and the worker in art are more like each other than either is like any one else.

Indeed as processes of mind in the worker science and art are much the same; both occupy themselves with a precise study of facts; in both man seeks to interpret and reconstruct nature after patterns of his own; both, in the pursuit of truth, rise above the tumult of the hour to serene and lasting aims.

ANY one whose need it is to strive for something perfect, something noble in itself without regard to any transient utility, one whose thoughts are bent on truth or beauty and not on the market, may be said to be of the artist type, whether he be called artist, scientist, poet, scholar, craftsman or teacher.

SCIENCE steps more assuredly than art, but its path is narrower; it cannot deal with life in its fulness. And so the humanistic studies—history, literature, psychology, sociology—can be sciences only as to detail; when they interpret life largely they are arts.

But indeed all science becomes art when it passes to the construction of truth.

THAT part of the progress of knowledge that interests most minds and affords the main field for discussion is not science, properly speaking, not the discovery of facts as such (about which there is very little to be said), but the art which is based on the facts, the theories and arguments by which it is endeavored to build up a system of ideal truth. Take a work on primitive man; how meager, when you sift it out, is the knowledge—a few tools, drawings and fragments of bone—how ample the structure imagination has built upon it!

TO arrive at abstract formulas is indeed one aim of science, but surely not the only one. To illuminate the concrete object is an equal need. "All theory is gray," especially if you separate it from the bright detail. Science, then, is not in this regard so very far from art, which is not all bright detail, but abstracts in a way of its own.

WHILE science seeks to discover a fact or relation which can be shown to all by experiment, art aims to express a personal vision of truth which can be shared by sympathy. One minimizes personality, the other exalts it. Yet they overlap in dealing with human life, for here the facts themselves are personal and experience becomes sympathy. Are the maxims of La Rochefoucauld science or art? And how about William James's psychology?

THE man of science, like the artist, may easily have more facts than he can use. Both seek the one fact out of a million that will illuminate their idea. Both find that it is rarely to be had without research.

THE test of truth in art is authenticity, that is, something in the work itself by which we judge that it expresses faithfully a real vision of the artist, very much as we judge of the truth of a witness by his face and bearing. A portrait by Holbein, a novel by W. D. Howells, a poem by Robert Frost, is authentic. And in science this test is by no means absent, since the sciences of life, especially, including the social, consist largely of description, the guaranty of which is the credibility of the observer.

SCIENCE, because it is more separable from personality, tends to be more anonymous, and can never be as prolific in fames as art is. Compare Newton with Shakespeare, Galileo with Dante or Michelangelo. Newton and Galileo are only names, familiar enough because they are on the lists of great men, but without rich meaning; what they contributed we have absorbed in another way. But the poets and painters and sculptors are alive still, in a unique and personal body of work which we can know only by knowing them. The world of literature and art has hundreds of names, each of which, to people of some culture, is an indispensable key to life.

PHILOSOPHY may be either science or art, or both, or neither. There is a sort that is impersonal, verifiable and cumulative, a large view of science, good to build on but not otherwise of much interest; another that is personal and of a speculative beauty, a third that is perhaps neither enduring nor beautiful, but influential for a particular state of thought.

ART colors science in unsuspected ways. There are formulas, like "trial and error" which gain vogue not because they are precise (this one is not) but because of an attractive sound and flow, a suggestiveness faintly poetic.

The Fallibility of Scientific Groups

SCIENCE is knowledge that is verifiable and cumulative, that can be established to the satisfaction of an expert group and endure as the basis of new acquisitions. But it is not easy to test this, since much that seems to an expert group verified and enduring may in the end prove transitory.

It is with science as elsewhere; the premises of thought, being common to a group, escape scrutiny, and so, by the most rigorous methods, the common error may be propagated indefinitely. No group is a trustworthy critic of its own premises. The men of the past thought they proved a world of things we regard as nonsense, and we cannot know how much of our own science will turn out to be of the same sort. Some results are permanent, but only time reveals which they are.

It is perhaps not sufficiently understood that nineteen twentieths of what men of science write, and what the public takes for science, is not such but an overflow of speculative discussion not necessarily less biased or more grounded than any other matter of the kind. No doubt this has a scientific value in that from the flood of conjecture fruitful hypotheses may emerge, but in the meantime all men should know that it *is* conjecture.

Scientific men are almost as eager to believe as the religious. Their doctrine differs from that of the church mainly in having a confessed obligation to show, sooner or later, that it consists with verifiable fact.

"Our facts will endure," you say, "though our theory is tentative." True; but is there any test of what is a fact except that it endures? What we have taken for granted or striven to prove appears to us to be fact; unfamiliar or unwelcome facts seem theoretical.

Verification is the assent of competent minds, not of the public. When you get beyond precise and easily repeated experiment it involves interpretation and is never unquestionable. A. R. Wallace got into serious trouble by attempting to prove, on a bet, that the surface of the earth was curved. The referee gave him the money, I believe, but the other man was never convinced. It all comes back to the verdict of the expert group, which is the best guide we have, but not infallible.

No wonder the plain people distrust "science" and cling in spite of it to cherished beliefs. It shows their good sense. What honest and thoughtful student expects that more than a small part of the contemporary speculation that reputable men proclaim as truth will be believed a century hence?

But evolution, you say, is no longer a speculation. It has proved the key to a hundred tangles, and is solving more every day. Yes, but you cannot expect the plain man to know all that. He judges by what he can see and by the credibility of the witnesses, of which he may have a poor opinion. He sees that many professed men of science are no less partisans, propagandists and followers of fads than other people, and draws his own conclusions.

THE group disciplines its members, but who will discipline the group?

Skirmishes on the Border

THE first step toward clear thinking about social or human knowledge, as compared with material or spatial knowledge, is to recognize that the former rests eventually upon sympathetic understanding of the acts of men, and can never be exact or mensurative in the sense that material knowledge can be. There are exact *processes* connected with social knowledge—statistics, behavior tests and the like—but these are secondary, aids to comparison and interpretation; the primary perceptions remain sympathetic, and the measurements get their social meaning from these. In spatial science, on the other hand, the primary perceptions are those of space and time and give rise to a sort of knowledge essentially measurable.

THE study and measurement of behavior, the outside of life, is a fruitful and promising method, but the idea of a human science consisting wholly of such study, without sympathetic observation of the mind, is, I think, only mystification. Outside and inside, consciousness and behavior, mutually complement and interpret each other. They cannot be disjoined without denaturing both.

SOCIAL investigation calls for a habit of mind unlike that of spatial science, and it is rare that men trained in the latter do sound work in it. Their precise and circumscribed sense of fact tends to incapacitate them for that sympathetic grasp of complex human conditions which is the prime need in social studies. They are apt to develop some particularistic doctrine which they elaborate with a great show of precision and imagine to be science—as some followers of Galton have attempted to inflate the study of heredity (most important in its place) into a science of society.

THE physical scientist approaching social studies sees that there are no such standards as he has been used to, and is apt to suppose that there are no standards at all, and to write with remarkable ignorance as to what has been done and consequent superficiality in his own work. Not a few appear to think that a little exact research in their own field entitles them to a plenary license of the imagination in others.

Nothing wilder, sometimes, than a laboratory man escaped from his instruments.

IT is true that we need more scientific method in politics, but to commit our public life to laboratory scientists, rather than to lawyers, business men, journalists and the like, as has been suggested, would get us into worse trouble than we have now. Our present rulers have at least a working familiarity with social processes; they know something of how the human world actually goes; laboratory scientists, as such, have not.

THE physical sciences and the sciences of life may some day be unified, but the actual gulf between them as regards ascertained principles is greater than is commonly understood. From the standpoint of nineteenth century physics there is no reason why there should be a world of life at all. But we observe that there is, and that it has an order of its own, including growth, development, organization, evolution, society, mind. The direct study of these is the only basis for the vital sciences. But this is so difficult and the scientific mind so full of physics that we have not yet got rid of analogical conceptions and method.

IF the vital and physical sciences are ever merged it may turn out that the latter have as much to learn from the former as vice versa. Instead of immutable physical laws being found to dominate life, it may appear that the supposed immutable laws of physics are in reality vital and flexible.

Pseudo-Science

WORK having an appearance of science but radically unsound flourishes in the social field chiefly because of popular interest in that field and the consequent flocking into it of those who lack the requisite insight and training. Some of these are real scientists in other fields; many have had no technical training and are not aware that they need it; some have training but lack good sense; nearly all make a show of precise method while lax in their assumptions.

MUCH would-be social science seeks to dodge the mental and emotional processes in which society consists, to circumvent them, find them superfluous, arrive at social truth without them. This is pseudo-science; in the end it will not work; these phenomena are nature; there is no substitute; if we are to have a science it must advance through them, not around them.

PSEUDO-SCIENCE is often honest. A great deal of it arises from a well-meant attempt to carry over into human subjects (psychology, sociology, education, literature) the exact methods of spatial science without perceiving where the conditions of the two kinds of knowledge are different.

IF psychology is the most copious fountain of pseudo-science this is because it concerns our inmost and secret desires. *Populus vult decipi*, and the supply meets the demand.

Perception

AFTER all the primary thing in any science is perception, a mind gifted and trained to absorb a certain sort of facts. Apart from this no method is of the least use. In social science perception calls for sympathetic contact with the people concerned. You will know nothing worth while about the labor question unless you are humanly familiar with workingmen. Not a few students work only in studies or laboratories, supposing their method to be objective when it is only blind.

I FIND that the aptest students of sociology are usually young men or women who have had to make their way through life in a rough-and-tumble manner, as agents, factory hands, reporters, school teachers and the like. Some of our ablest men began as preachers; indeed the conduct of a parish is an excellent training, and two or three years of it a better preparation for social science than the same time in a laboratory.

PERCEPTION of a scientific sort is the work of a continuing group: there is always a tradition without which you do not know what to look for. And however crude and inchoate the tradition may be this is as true of social science as of any other.

Diagrams and Statistics

IN the study of human relations diagrams and mechanical analogies often supplant truth rather than reveal it. You say, "How plain that makes it!" But the thing that is plain is the mechanical idea, not the human. Helpful comparisons, as a rule, are those which illuminate complex human situations by simpler ones of the same order; as you may, for some purposes, liken a state to a group of boys.

USE diagrams, by all means, use classifications, use maps, curves, statistics—and forget them! These are methods of manipulating the material, as they are in botany and zoology. But the materials themselves are living wholes which can only be apprehended by a trained sympathy in contact with them. And when you have reached your conclusions, no presentation of them is adequate that does not restore the facts to their human reality.

NOTHING more illuminating or more fallacious than statistics. If the underlying material is trustworthy they may reveal its meaning; but numerical exactitude is often the only thing scientific about them.

THE movement of social life in large masses is in great part impelled by mere inertia. There are many currents of somewhat mechanical motion that can be measured as to mass and direction by statistics, and when they meet the course of their resultants can sometimes be predicted by the same method. But in new situations a real intelligence is called into play and a fresh synthesis made which is more than a mechanical resultant and cannot be predicted by statistics alone. No method will work here except that of embracing the situation in your mind and, by an act of creative intelligence, anticipating the outcome—much as you would anticipate the conduct of an individual by putting yourself wholeheartedly in his place.

A STUDENT who leans upon arithmetic, who is afraid of any line of thought which he cannot test by figures, who does not see that there are quite other criteria in this field, can have only an ancillary function in social science.

Traits of Sociology

ALL books dealing largely with human questions are speculative, those abounding in statistics and laboratory observations as much so as any. You may always see, if you look closely, vast chasms bridged by conjecture: we know so little that it cannot be otherwise. Not method, chiefly, but sagacity, insight, breadth of knowledge, humble honesty and real love of truth are our guaranty for the value of these speculations; and we must judge whether we can trust our author very much as we do in the case of the doctor, lawyer or plumber.

Exact science attracts by the prospect of tangible and lasting truth; it appeals to our need of something sure and imperishable. It gives the discoverer a personal claim upon the human mind of all time, which must use his results. Social truth is not so distinct and appropriable, not so surely eternal. The thinker cannot be so certain that he has found God or informed man. But he is reasonably sure of increasing insight into a realm where even tentative knowledge is of incomparable human interest.

Since the facts of sociology are those of personality and human change, and since these are precisely what the men of other sciences are taught to eliminate, it would be strange if they did not regard this science with distrust.

Sociology makes us more at home in the world of men, as botany or geology does in the world of rocks or plants. Life is no longer a wilderness of alarming shapes, but an orderly process, even when dangerous or repulsive. We see something of what is going on and begin to adjust ourselves intelligently to it. We can collect social facts in the same spirit as we do botanical or geological.

It tends to cure pessimism not by promising a bright future but by showing each one's life as member of a greater process. Our fate, then, is not casual, but organic, dramatic, perhaps tragic, at any rate reconcilable with thought.

Human life as a whole is much like the particular enterprises that make it up: it is something that we may hope to work out successfully by constancy and intelligence. This intelligence, on a large scale, is social science.

We understand another person, in some measure, through the process of our own development, which is similar to his, enabling us to participate in his life and observe where it is like or unlike ours. It is the purpose of social science to extend our mental development and participation so as to embrace groups and processes in a similar way.

We hear it questioned whether sociology is a science or a philosophy. It is both, and an art also.

THERE is no enterprise more engaging to the intellect, the imagination and the sympathies than the intimate study of a village, a factory, a school, or other limited group, with a view to understanding its life and perhaps exerting some helpful influence upon it.

THE more involved with human life is the material of a science the more is breadth of humane culture a *sine qua non* of the student.

Two Ways of Organizing Life

TWO methods have been worked out in the course of evolution by which life organizes itself to deal with the conditions it has to meet. The first is the method of hereditary patterns. Nobody knows just how these patterns are formed and altered, but the process is slow and they give rise to a comparatively fixed organization, transmitted through the germ-plasm, appearing as instinct, and dominant in the plants and lower animals. An example is the ready-made system by which the honey-bee, specialized as queen, drones and workers, finds and collects wax, builds the comb, produces and cares for its young. This is wonderful, but too fixed and limited for the highest uses.

The second is the system of plastic and more or less intelligent organization, the patterns of which are carried by language or other social symbols. To achieve this, heredity loses its fixed patterns of behavior and becomes a raw material of indeterminate powers which can be shaped by habit into the plastic organization. This organization consists, in the individual, of a system of habits formed during his life and ceasing at his death, which enables him to carry on those activities which his particular time and social function call for; his timely death ensuring that he does not carry them on too long, making way for a new individual capable of acquiring new habits. As for example a locomotive engineer, who may need to be replaced in the next generation by an electrician. In a larger view the higher organization appears as a social system—families, schools, churches, governments, arts, sciences, industries— which trains and uses the engineers and other specialized individuals, and in so doing, through the medium of habit, develops, guides and organizes the indeterminate powers carried by the germ-plasm.

We have thus an enormously complex and very adaptable system, using three processes: social transmission through language, habit-forming in the nerve cells of the individual, and heredity through the germ-plasm. It has innumerable patterns stored up in language and other records but is not bound to use any one of them; selects and adapts those it needs, increases them by invention, and gives them a temporary organization and efficacy in the habits of the individual. This is the human way.

I should now add that there are three kinds of scientists who busy themselves with the three processes: biologists, who specialize on the germ-plasm, psychologists, who deal mainly with the organization of the individual through habit, and sociologists, who are concerned with groups and the social process. And each of these, as a rule, is immutably convinced that the subject of his studies is more fundamental and more generally worth while than that of the others.

The Organization of Freedom

VERY much as the animal or fixed organization of life was gradually supplanted by the human or plastic, so, within the latter, there is growing up an organization based upon personal mobility and choice instead of upon position transmitted from father to son. Modern communication, popular education, democracy, place-finding devices and the like may all be regarded as phases of this change. In so far as the new system is achieved it will have advantages over the old—of energy and adaptability—similar to those of the human system over the animal.

"Heredity or Environment"

THIS is a scholastic or quasi-metaphysical dilemma which does not correspond to the facts of human life and has less meaning the more you study it. Neither heredity nor environment has any distinct existence during the development of the individual. The former is an antecedent rather than a present factor, while environment is in great measure the human organism itself, every part of which is environmental to every other part.

Part Five

Academic

A Soft Job

ONE winter day, when I was a young instructor, I took a long walk into the country, in the course of which I got a ride from a farmer who was driving a pair of bobsleds. We talked a little, and on his asking what sort of work I did I told him I was a teacher in the University. He thought about this a while and then said, "Well, I don't blame any man for getting his living easy if he can *do* it."

An Art?

TEACHING is an art and ought to be practiced in joy. It *is* joyous if one can find himself in it, can teach with freedom, with love of the matter, in a friendly spirit and without strain.

THE situation of a professor fosters self-consciousness, sometimes, no doubt, to the point of ridiculous egotism. It tends to the histrionic, and the men who win large classes usually have a knack of dramatizing themselves and their subject. The student may laugh a little and say, "X thinks a lot of himself," but he elects the course because it makes knowledge human.

IN 1897 I heard Joseph Jefferson talk on The Actor and his Art. He made much of what he called the "art of reproduction," of acting always with the spontaneity one felt at first, not falling into routine.

THE teacher also is a dramatist, who must conceive his subject freshly for each performance, and he will hardly do this unless he himself sees something in it he never saw before. Perfunctoriness is the death of any art.

The Day's Work

THE life of a professor has no such freedom from conflict as people suppose. He has to contend with students, with colleagues, with officials, sometimes with parents; and with what energy he has left he contends with his subject. If not insecure in his job he is uncertain about promotion. Courtesy prevails, but inwardly it is a strenuous game like another. Many are anxious, worried, irritable.

TEACHING compels you to principles. You have to discover what is that solid and rounded idea that can be tossed from mind to mind like a ball, fitting every one's fingers. And the peril of it is that your ideas become indeed solid and rounded and tossable—and dead.

WHATEVER else students do or do not get they will always get your attitudes—as open-minded or dogmatic, adventurous or conventional, confident or suspicious, self-absorbed or appreciative of their personalities. For the last they are always grateful.

THE function of a college teacher divides itself into two not unequal parts; to help half his students educate themselves and to hinder the other half from getting easy credits.

The crime side of life, with its suspicions, resentments and reprisals, is present in almost every class.

ONE of the most depressing things I do is to go to faculty meeting. How much more edifying are students than professors!

The true reason, no doubt, is that I do not shine on these occasions.

The Eloquent Man

A MAN, a mature student, came to me to be cured of eloquence. He said, "I am an eloquent man," with the air of one revealing an obscure defect. He had been employed as a temperance lecturer and the like to a degree that he felt was injurious. By renouncing these habits and devoting himself to serious study he eventually recovered and is now the much respected president of a college.

Formalism

FORMALISM prevails because it is the line of least resistance, easy for the teacher, easy for the student. How comfortable for both to deal only with patterns and systems which all can learn and be answerable for at examinations! Live truth is a most troublesome thing in a classroom.

Human teaching calls for an expense of spirit on each individual possible only when there are few of them. The teacher is the dividend the students the divisor, and when they are many the quotient is routine.

Is a good text-book possible, or is a text-book in its nature just one of our machines for mass production? Certainly the product, as we find it in the student's mind, has much the same relation to knowledge as our factory furniture has to art. And the things thought essential to a text-book—impersonality, numbered and labeled paragraphs, an obvious style, test questions at the end of the chapter—are they not death?

The Dark Ages, it seems, was a time when people read text-books and thought they were literature.

IN educational research formalism flourishes as a pseudo-scientific striving for precision in matters which can be precise only as they are denatured. "Let us make education an exact science."

IF you must choose it is better that students should not understand than that fine things should be made coarse in the telling. Let them become vaguely aware of something to divine and aspire toward.

IT was a formidable criticism when a student said, "They do not know I am here." In fact no teacher or official does, in most cases, become aware of the student as a human whole; he is known only by detached and artificial functions.

Heritage and Spontaneity

WHICH shall guide education, the heritage of the past or the spontaneity of the young?

We cannot dispense with the social heritage nor with our need to select out of it what we may think worth passing on. But nothing is rightly passed on except as it is discovered and appropriated in freedom, as a boy discovers and appropriates the heritage of craft in a chest of tools. The young must desire and experiment before they can possess. We can only offer.

A thoughtful mind needs to build a world of its own and cannot take yours ready-made. To have faith in human nature and continence to let it alone is often the best and hardest service.

THE young see themselves more naturally in one another's eyes than in those of an instructor, and so the matter they are supposed to study will hardly appear socially real to them except as they see it in informal discussions among themselves.

The Passing Current

IF I stand at the classroom door and seek the eye of each student as they come in I get a human sense of them that makes it easier to talk to them. A strange crowd facing you is oppressive.

ON certain mornings the lecturer, watching the faces flow past, may think, "This is God; the real thing, no myth; in these individualities and this humanity is the passing current of that continuing and inscrutable life."

COLLEGE students are not the homogeneous crowd that some imagine. As in other societies, there is a dominant type or form that more or less imposes itself upon the whole, but underneath there are variants, many of them maladjusted and more or less psychopathic. In the eye of each, if you look for it, you may see an individual spirit, a self, often only partly at home with its fellows.

The Chair

A LECTURE, like any public speaking, is an adventure; it is like being thrown overboard, a sink-or-swim matter. Without a bold spirit there is no holding an audience, though you spoke like Solomon. If you falter they are bored. One must himself be aroused a little, must go beyond his outline and say what he never thought of saying.

One sometimes thinks, "How crude my lectures were ten years ago: I wonder how I got them across." But it is spontaneity and conviction that holds students, and these may well have been greater ten years ago than now.

Nothing more pitiable than one trying to interest a roomful of students in something he doesn't care for himself.

If I don't tell the whole truth, so far as I know it, it is because I do not know what you are looking for. Ask me and you will get it.

A speaker must see or feel a visible or tangible form of what he has to say; it must exist for him in the round and as a whole, and the fitness of each word and thought must be judged in the sense of that whole. His must be an organic, not a linear, progression.

Under the more intense feeling of his public that one has when preparing to lecture his matter takes on a colloquial distinctness that it might never get in writing. One feels that every idea must be lucid and every word get across. But inaccuracies of fact and inference are easily overlooked.

The reason that a speaker who reads his discourse is apt to be ineffectual is that he does not easily put himself into it. Not having to *think* his ideas his mind wanders from them, he loses aggressive unity with his thought, and is no longer the assailant, the leader, drawing all eyes, but the clerk of a forgotten mood. It is a good plan, when you have to read a paper, to say something extempore first, in order to get a natural start.

Men of a strong dramatic sense, however, can put themselves into a manuscript and at the same time profit by its considered expression. Diffuse, demonstrative people usually do better when they read.

The ready speaker has a strong flow of weak language; he takes at least three times as many words to say a given thing as in careful writing. Clergymen, politicians and professors are apt to write as they talk, and hence badly.

When preparing a speech it is not well to write out a version and learn it—that is too narrow a track, and if you get out of it you are lost—but to prepare several versions, permitting a sense of freedom, as of one who knows the country and can choose his road. You may compose what you hope will be telling passages, and retain the option to use them or not as the unforeseeable fitness of the moment may decree.

American Universities

AN American university is something new under the sun; not merely, perhaps not chiefly, an institution of learning, but a vast social and economic enterprise, a struggling organ of confused democracy, striving to grow, to make good, to find a popular function and pecuniary support. It may have diluted the intellectual heritage of the past, but has by no means thrown it away, and shows vigorous though problematic energies peculiar to the present.

THE universities, being permanent and ambitious institutions, organizing their alumni—including most of the highly trained men and women of the country—about those social and athletic interests that appeal so strongly to Americans, may become, if they are not already, the most powerful influence in our society, excepting the economic system. Once the handmaid of the Church, they have now, as regards intellectual leadership, supplanted it.

A GATHERING of alumni from all over the land is discussing plans to "boost" the University. Why? What makes that seem worth while to these busy and skeptical men?

Most of them are "doers" who enjoy the exertion of power for its own sake and feel vaguely that this is a worthy object. They believe the University stands for culture and a better life, although just what those are it would perhaps puzzle them to say. Their more definite views relate largely to athletics, which they see as an evident contribution. You might fairly say that they have faith in God and in the University as working out his will.

EVERY institution suffers from the sins of every other; and so our universities struggle as they can with deficiencies left by the family, the school, the economic system and the general trend of life, contributing, no doubt, a few errors of their own. It is all one problem.

IT is the chief weakness of these institutions that they too easily allow values, pecuniary and other, to flow in upon them from the general current, instead of creating values of their own. You say, "It is the market." But *whose* market?

THERE is a function of a quasi religious nature performed by a few experts but followed in spirit by the whole university world, serving indeed as a symbol to arouse in the students and in the alumni certain congregate and hieratic emotions. I refer, of course, to football.

The Campus

THE common spirit of a university easily pervades all comers. Control this and you can impart anything—high thought, plain living, generous ideals and endeavors, the culture of beauty and manners, truth, worship, what you will. But who can bind the sweet influences of the Pleiades?

IT is assumed that the student is wrong when he does not behave as the faculty would like to have him, but the truth is that the two groups have somewhat different interests, and he is not wholly mistaken in thinking that complete docility would be to his disadvantage. The faculty, moving in their own ruts and, like other men, somewhat uninspired, endeavor to impose what seems from their standpoint a proper scheme of college life. The students, on the other hand, feel that a mode of living which is rounded and human now and a sound preparation for the future is sometimes incompatible with the faculty demands. A conflict of wits thus arises, good-natured for the most part, and so long as this goes on we must expect that the ethics of conflict, which always justify deceiving the enemy, will to some extent prevail.

The campus is a social system in itself, not foreseen by anybody, and in great part set up by the students in a groping endeavor to develop a mode of life congenial to tastes they have already formed in their families and home towns. It does not escape the general American current.

I APPROVE the student who, reacting against the excessive and irreconcilable claims made upon him, listens deferentially to advice but resolves to set his own value upon the opportunities offered and arrange his life accordingly.

I SHOULD advise a boy who is ambitious for culture to go to college, if he can, for the sake of leisure, books and possibly-inspiring persons. The curriculum is not to be taken too seriously; let him follow a plan of his own, preferring courses in which he is encouraged to work in his own way. All depends upon himself; college is merely a not unfavorable condition, and if he cannot go he may do as well without it.

THE indifference to social problems shown by most American students is that of the comfortable class from which they come. The proportion of our people who can, and hence do, live in undisturbed ignorance of such matters, is larger than in other countries. That there is so little radical ferment indicates a rather dull and self-complacent civilization. The zeal to suppress what little there is, though stupid, should probably be encouraged as a possible incentive to rebellion. If you can stage a fight the young will begin to take notice.

AMERICAN students have some of the virtues of aristocracy—magnanimity, courage, self-respect, group discipline, fair play (among themselves), sometimes engaging manners. Possibly they may yet proceed to *noblesse oblige* and the finer kinds of ambition.

Scholars and Administrators

IT is a peculiarity of American universities, incident to their expansion, that much of their activity resembles that of aggressive business. The administrative officers who have this activity in charge receive higher pay than the scholars, and in some cases appear more imbued by the commercial spirit than the academic. Their lives may or may not offer to the student any argument to change the ideals of success he has brought with him from the world outside. The scholars may even seem a kind of caged and subdued animals whose exotic attractions are proclaimed and exploited by their keepers. Since they have, at any rate, less immediate power and prestige than the administrators it is difficult for them not to feel a certain inferiority, and men who appear to have executive ability (especially if they see no prospect of high distinction in scholarship) are under pressure to abandon teaching and research for administration, as they frequently do.

It is conducive to intellectual achievement in our universities to be known as incapacitated for anything else. One may be thankful for a poor voice and hesitating address, a perturbable and withdrawing disposition, a general appearance of scholarly inefficiency. It will retard his promotion, but he has some chance of really doing something in the long run.

"F is a man of genius and a noble personality: let him prepare and deliver a eulogy on our late benefactor." Scarcely any one understands that to require a man of this type to do a kind of thing he doesn't believe in not only wastes his energy but vitiates his whole nature. It is a kind of poison you make him take. The administrator is accustomed to making any sort of perfunctory speech the occasion calls for, and doesn't see why any one else shouldn't do the same.

That mobilizing of the mind to meet and sway the minds of other men, involved in the conduct of affairs, blunts a sense of fine truth. The administrator is the death of the artist.

The learned world is full of active men—presidents, deans, heads of large departments, officers of Foundations—eminent, admirable, indispensable men, good fellows, too, but not men of science, not in any strict sense. Show me an important discovery or a first-rate book by men of this sort! (I can think of two or three that might pass.) They are mostly like women whose bearing days, if any, are over and who have taken to managing Children's Aid Societies. The real man of science is pregnant, brooding, usually unfit for administration. He may teach, if you let him teach what is on his mind, but not manage. Although indifferently paid, and without prestige with the public (which commonly identifies eminence with office) he has a good life and is sure of the kind of recognition he cares for.

Good administrators are paid more than good scholars not because they are rarer (they are perhaps equally rare) but because scholars are not in the same degree sought and discriminated on the market. Administrators are standard commodities in the commercial system, while scholars have only such pecuniary value as the administrators create by their demand. The latter desire that their institutions should have scholars of high repute, but since, like all men of affairs, they are concerned with immediate values, and since high excellence in a scholar is usually slow of recognition and lacks immediate value, they are not so eager to seek it out as greatly to enhance its price. Availability is what they want, an all-around competence and leadership which includes good intellectual standing, attractive personality, and aptitude for teaching, as well as practical shrewdness and initiative. The administrator sees his man as a focus of present light and power, much of which is reflected upon the institution. Rare gifts have, as a rule, little effect upon the market unless, by some striking achievement, they have acquired an advertising value.

I do not know that scholars are paid too little, as compared, say, with mechanics, clergymen or farmers, but that in institutions of learning they should be rated lower than another class seems somewhat ironical.

The administrator is personally combatant and must keep the aggressiveness and the reserve energy required for his function. This is hardly possible to the scholar, who must preserve the fineness of his mind, spend himself upon unseen contests and appear a poor thing before the world.

It is usually possible to make a fair administrator out of a scholar, just as you can make over a touring car into a tolerable truck. The main thing is to suppress all irregular and exhausting excursions of the mind and use the energy thus saved for system and poise. You lower the gear and stiffen the frame.

Genius on the Faculty

It is strange that we have so few men of genius on our faculties; we are always trying to get them. Of course they must have undergone the regular academic training (say ten years in graduate study and subordinate positions) and be gentlemanly, dependable, pleasant to live with, and not apt to make trouble by urging eccentric ideas.

Institutions and genius are in the nature of things antithetical, and if a man of genius is found living contentedly in a university it is peculiarly creditable to both. As a rule professors, like successful lawyers or doctors, are just hard-working men of some talent.

IT is true in university life as elsewhere that early success, as distinguished from eventual fame, usually implies an opportunism scarcely compatible with genius.

Academic Freedom

IF academic thinkers do not influence life it is because they are feeble thinkers, not because their views are suppressed. Suppression is rarely attempted and would be easy to evade. The real trouble is in the process of selection, which, in universities as in all institutions, tends to elicit a somewhat mediocre and over-disciplined type of ability.

THE head of a department (whatever his own views) will seldom choose a man whose opinions, or whose mode of expressing them, are likely to discredit the department with the general administration. This does not bar radicals, if they are men of tact, but their radicalism seldom survives their success. The contentious radical, whatever his value, is by nature a free lance, not to be looked for in institutions.

IT might be supposed that the social teaching in a State university is guided by the democracy of the plain people who support it, or, possibly, by the capitalism of the trustees. In truth it is guided by neither, but chiefly by the opinion and emulation of an expert group of scholars extending through the learned institutions of the country. This is the audience to whom, in imagination, one submits his views.

IT is true that the universities are, in a sense, class institutions. They are accessible (with difficulty) to the children of the farming and laboring classes, but these children are seeking to escape from those classes and to enter the professional and business classes, to which nearly all the alumni belong. All the well-informed opinion and criticism influencing the institution comes from the same quarter. If the points of view of the farming interest and of the labor movement are competently presented, as they often are, it is because liberal minded presidents and professors see the university as the organ of the whole people, and pursue this ideal in the face of difficulty.

The Academic Outlook

A UNIVERSITY is among the most spacious and commanding situations on earth: commercial and political capitals are narrow and special compared with it. Here you may know any nation or class in the persons of the youth it has formed, and may set your own mark upon them. The currents of contemporary life, as well as those of traditional knowledge, gather here like wires at a central exchange.

Through students, who bring the spirit of a thousand neighborhoods, one can come into larger and more solid contact with American life than through the newspapers and magazines. The latter are more ruled by transient and superficial waves of thought, and a kind of emulation in up-to-dateness destroys their perspective. They give no adequate reflection of the conservatism, good faith, hopefulness and common-sense of the people.

A TEACHER is sustained by a noble institution as a singer's voice by an orchestra. It gives him assurance and function in a whole. To serve it may be a kind of worship.

Outing

I NEVER feel more that life is worth living than when struggling with winds and waters, and when resting afterward. Nature is sweet to overcome.

I have been camping a month. One lives in the work—cooking, camp-making, cutting balsam boughs for the beds, portaging and the like. I have had a few rather luminous thoughts, but the senses—eating and the anticipation of it, muscular activity, sunshine and chill—take up almost all of life.

Part Six

Human Nature

Is Human Nature Selfish?

La Rochefoucauld's Maxims, chiefly on self-love, are true, but portray, after all, only an aspect of human nature. Others, equally true, might be written on the generous impulses. The facts would be in great part the same, but shown in a different light. The pessimism is in his attitude. It is through an enlarged self-love, if you call it that, that the noblest things are done.

That we often find something not displeasing in the adversity of our best friends (thought to be his most cynical maxim) is merely, I suppose, because we are thus reminded of our own better state. If a friend has tuberculosis we may gloat a little over the soundness of our own lungs; but this does not prevent our grieving for him, and may even go with unselfish devotion. It is more shocking to be said than sinister in itself.

Indeed I should hardly call his sentences cynical. They are searching and a little gloomy, as from a disillusioned courtier, but not ungenerous.

The core of human nature is a social self. We are socially selfish or selfishly social as you please to look at it.

Self-Expression

The fuel that drives our engine is the self impulse, a certain ardor and craving to bring forth something of our own and make it work in the general life. In a given individual this is not far from a fixed quantity: no man who can put himself into mediocre things will do rare ones.

From this comes the chief advantage of retirement to a thinker. It is not so much that association interferes actively with his thoughts as that it appeases his sense of self-existence. In retirement the self presses for an outlet and pours itself into the one channel that is open.

ONLY self-expression gives us assurance, and when we cease from our usual modes of it we become restless, apprehensive, unsure of ourselves and life. We have no sense of power unless we are moving something. I often feel a kind of disintegration when I am released from my round of work, a sense of emptiness and dread as if I were falling into space. I am freest not when I am idle but in the intervals of a moderate activity. I need that to keep alive the sense of an active whole which gives me room to be free in.

IN order that the right shall be alive and fruitful for us we have to make an ambition of it, to connect it with active purpose, to enself it. If it is part of that work of art I am trying to make I shall take an interest in it.

It is true that salvation lies in escaping from a narrow self into the great life of humanity; yet neither the great life of humanity nor any other great thing will satisfy a productive spirit unless he can make of it something private and peculiar, something defiantly his own,—in short a self.

WE are indeed sponges to absorb the commonplace; but if one has character the commonplace will nourish that too and take its form. Great men have no better food than the rest of us, and often less of it.

INEQUALITY of wealth would be unimportant if it did not involve the denial of self-expression. The main thing is so to order life that each of us may have the materials out of which to make a healthy self.

IN life as in sports contests should be so numerous and so graded that every man has a chance to win honor in his class.

I LIKE to express myself cleanly, and like others to do the same; I would have each individual stand out unique and perspicuous, like a character in a play. I am sickened by the blurred, trivial, hurrying images of ourselves that we cast on the mind of the time.

The Looking-Glass Self

A SENSITIVE person is subject to erratic impulses springing from his imagination of what other people are thinking about him. Hence he needs to build up a firm idea of what he really is, so that he may be that, resist what is alien and escape affectation. Hence also the restfulness of being with those whom you know know you.

HIS self-consciousness is awakened and intimidated by strange people. It is fear in the dark. Every new person is a fresh glass in which he is impelled to see himself. Hardly a child comes into the house but he finds himself imagining how he appears to it and wishing to appear well.

SOME dislike to talk about themselves because it exposes them and awakens a disquieting self-consciousness. There are authors that do not like to see their own books before them on the shelf; it gives them a feeling as of sitting before a mirror. Much that may pass as modesty comes from a supersensitive self.

IT is well to limit yourself not only in your own mind but in the minds of others, that you may be free from inappropriate expectations. There is nothing more disastrous than to set up for something you are not, and be taken at your word.

NOTHING, says Epictetus, is more ruinous to good resolutions than publicity. One reason is that a project kept hid and private becomes identified with one's inmost and secret self. It is sweet for that reason, and the more likely to be cherished. If we boast of our treasure it becomes vulgar to ourselves and we are soon sick of it. Moreover to talk about our high projects is to ask sympathy for them. We either get this or we do not. If we do not we are discouraged; if we do we form the habit of depending upon something which will usually fail us.

When I was a boy about seventeen I heard a preacher in Denver say that an idea cherished in secret until it became a passion acquired great power. This appeared to me to be true, and I have carried it about with me ever since, considerably, I believe, to my advantage.

I MIGHT have saved myself much distraction if I had been less shy about asking advice. I did not understand that people rather like to give it and can often think better for others than for themselves. It is particularly salutary in matters involving self-consciousness, so that you cannot see them dispassionately—as when one is in doubt whether to ask for a raise in his pay. However there are few worse habits than that of depending on advice.

VANITY, like sexual impulse, gives rise to needless self-reproach. Why be ashamed of anything so human? What, indeed, should we be without it? All it needs is to be turned into large and wholesome channels.

A shrinking life will not destroy it but merely give it timid and petty shapes. It is better to accept it, somewhat ironically, perhaps, as we might a slightly ridiculous member of our family.

It is not only persons whose eyes we cannot meet when we have acted meanly. We are ashamed before the nobleness of intimate books: they look the other way and will not welcome us.

If you attempt converse with Y you perceive that he suffers from uneasy feelings about the impression he may be making on you. He resents not passing for as great a man as he would like to think he is. While he is genial at times you are never secure from covert brutalities or insults arising from his chagrins. He is fundamentally a right-seeking and even magnanimous man, but never simple and serene, nor can you be so in his company.

We need an ideal of ourselves that is an ideal of being rather than of seeming. But how can we form such an ideal when it is through our seeming, reflected to us from others, that we discern our being? It is the problem of the artist before nature: he must see precisely, and make of what he sees something he has not seen. Out of the confused glimpses the world gives back to us we must form a picture of what we are and can be.

We are urged to be ourselves and affect nothing. But how can a young man be himself when he is not sure what he is, when he has dozens of beginning selves not established in habit? We have no means of knowing our self except by observing how others respond to it, and we can be assuredly ourselves only when we have had long experience of a certain kind of response. Affectation is pretending something in order to impress others. To escape it we must either be very dull, so as not to perceive others' ideas of us, or constructive, so as to make a stable ideal of our own out of them. As we grow older we usually become a little of both, and so outgrow the affectation of youth.

Nothing is truer to experience or more wholesome to recognize than that the impression we make comes from what we are, in inmost desire and habit, and not from what we may try to seem to be. Our souls are not much hidden.

Possessions

AVOID possessions, say the ascetic philosophers, so as to be free in spirit. Many of us in fact accumulate recklessly, not perceiving that everything a man owns owns him. But certain possessions are functional, and we must have them to play our part. If wife, children, reputation, property, ambitions, belong to our job we may not refuse the risk of having them, though we may perhaps insure our souls in something less precarious.

GIVE a man a secure position and you will note an access of self-confidence and ease of intercourse: he feels the social order bearing him up. It will go far to make a very common man a gentleman. One whose self is established may forget it.

ONE is a distincter man if he can root himself somewhere and grow with the neighborhood; he gains in depth, significance, flavor, absorbs a local tradition and spirit, sees himself as part of a continuing whole. If this is no longer possible to our shifting life perhaps we can make America itself a neighborhood and absorb that.

The Material "I"

NOTHING better shows the human self than the fact that we make an "I" of any material object which embodies, for the time being, our interest and purpose in the game of life; as a golf player will say "I am in the creek beyond the hole." And if we call the body "I" it is only when we enter that too in the game, as when one says, "I am the tallest man here."

There is a curious instance of this in the early letters of Samuel Butler, when he was a New Zealand sheep herder. He says, "I have to dip within three months and thoroughly clean myself, or forfeit my £100 and a similar fine for every three months during which I continue scabby."

On A Remark of Dr. Holmes

DOCTOR HOLMES says that six persons take part in every conversation between John and Thomas: 1. The real John, known only to his Maker. 2. John's ideal John, never the real one and often very unlike him. 3. Thomas's ideal John. And, of course, three Thomases.* The matter is really more complicated, and one would not need to go beyond every-day experience to find at least twelve persons participating, six

* The Autocrat of the Breakfast Table, No. III.

on each side. Suppose, to animate the exposition, we change the sex and have Alice, who has a new hat, meet Angela, who has a new dress. We may have, 1. The real Alice, "known only to her Maker." 2. Her idea of herself; e.g. "I (Alice) look well in this hat." 3. Her idea of Angela's idea of her; e.g. "Angela thinks I look well in this hat." 4. Her idea of what Angela thinks she thinks of herself; e. g. "Angela thinks I am proud of my looks in this hat." 5. Angela's actual idea of Alice; e.g. "Alice looks ugly in that hat." 6. Angela's idea of what Alice thinks of herself; e. g. "Alice thinks she is stunning in that hat." And of course six analogous phases of Angela and her dress.

Any one of these types of ideal persons might be of momentous importance. Thus under 6 would come, let us say, the German idea of what Americans would think of the sinking of Americans on the Lusitania by a German submarine. Indeed this case is more complicated than any of those given, and might justify an enlargement of our array of ideal persons. It actually involves the German idea of the American idea of the German idea of Americans—as manifested by the Germans supposing that they could sink the Lusitania without the Americans effectively resenting the contemptuous idea of themselves (Americans) which they would as-scribe to the Germans on account of this act. This error on the part of the Germans possibly lost them the war. Thus our imaginations reverberate echoes of echoes of echoes of personality, for which we listen so eagerly that the last and faintest may guide momentous decision.

SOCIETY is an interweaving and interworking of mental selves. I imagine your mind, and especially what your mind thinks about my mind, and what your mind thinks about what my mind thinks about your mind. I dress my mind before yours and expect that you will dress yours before mine. Whoever cannot or will not perform these feats is not properly in the game.

On Certain Sentiments

LOVE leads to strife, and is ever seeking to allay it. Strife wins love power, but is ever making it weaker. Without strife love would be formless; without love strife would be fruitless.

THERE is a community of hatred. Hatred floods your mind with the idea of the one you hate. Your thought reflects his, and you act in his spirit. The hateful things he did to you you do to him. You feel a passion to equal or excel him in hatred: it is a union as intimate as love. So hating men and hating nations whirl about in an embrace of hateful passion which impels them to a common destruction. If you wish to be like your enemy, to be wholly his, open your mind and hate him.

KINDNESS is wisdom, but our force does not always suffice for it. It is a form of power, and scarcely more to be had for the wishing than the muscular. Indeed all love is from a surplus of life which we may easily dissipate.

IT is good fortune to be so placed that you *can* forget antagonism and see men as brothers. To have found your work and to see your way clear ahead is the main thing. If a man is living his life he should have no great difficulty in loving his neighbors.

"LOVE your enemies," if you can do it, is shrewd practice. It saves you from the wear and tear of evil passions, while your opposition will be all the more effective for being good-natured.

TO think kindly thoughts of your interlocutor is not only an amiable habit but a cure for embarrassment. It gives one a faint sense of benefaction which is fortifying.

WHEN a man has attained the habit of appearing kindly he has lost one of his chief motives for being so, and often relapses into selfishness.

PEOPLE who live in a narrow circle are kind, perhaps, but rarely just. Only an open and varied life educates us to share many points of view, and so to become capable of justice.

JUSTICE requires sympathy, since it must understand; but may be impaired by too much. No one whose action affects large numbers can afford to imagine minutely how they are affected. A general must not think too much of the wounded. A just view is a work of art, possible only by selection of details.

EASE and extreme hardship both tend to selfishness. The life most favorable to sympathy is one which includes a share of hardship but leaves times of relaxation when thought, by assimilating experience, may ripen into understanding.

It is more prudent to take away a man's life than to alienate his self-respect. If you let him live, leave him some reason for living well. A punished man, unless he can see his punishment as just and necessary, saves his self-respect in the only way possible, by defiance of the punitive agent and all it stands for.

The poor are right in resenting benefactions. "Benefits oblige and obligation is thraldom."*

The "Gregarious Instinct"

This is an invention of hedging individualists. It implies that a human nature generally insular has at a particular point a special social impulse, the alleged instinct. In truth the social tendencies of human nature are general and multiform, not specific and exceptional. We are social through and through.

Plans

Able men plan and strive not as being discontented now but because they need to continue that hope and sense of achievement they already have. They bring the future into the scene to animate the present. The same need to unify our thoughts that gives us a conscience also impels us to include the future in the present and work to a plan. To order our life by a purpose is a kind of righteousness.

Our plans are our working hopes and among our chief treasures. We need to husband them as we do our income, to use them moderately and to see to it that we do not fail of them in age. What worse prodigality than to dissipate our plans!

When one's self-respect is impaired by the present he may restore it by doing something for the future.

It is said that an unborn child, if it does not get nourishment otherwise, will draw it from the tissues of the mother—practically eat her up. There is something analogous in the voracity of a plan. It *will* thrive, though it has to engross the substance of the soul and finally destroy it. "Let a man beware how he proposes to himself any end."

---

* Hobbes

It is good to plan boldly not only because of the future but because it imparts an immediate elevation. Though my plan should never come to fruit I have the joy and hope of it, and the power, too, for the consciousness of living for large things adds to a man's stature and authority.

The impression we get of another comes not so much from what he is actually doing as from what we imagine him to be living for—his plans, his hopes, his faiths and loyalties.

One cannot plan too carefully, but it is well to do this disinterestedly, as if you were planning for some one else, not committing yourself to execution nor drawing in advance upon that fund of emotion which you will need when you come to act. There are no such wastes as those of the anticipative imagination.

Resolutions are a sort of voluntary constraint, as Odysseus had himself tied to the mast so he could not follow the sirens, but I doubt whether they are expedient. They are irksome, and no self-respecting man will keep them unless they seem right when he comes to act. It is enough to have thought out possible courses and to decide which to follow when you have to.

Anticipation

The children have a way of singing, "To-morrow, tomorrow," when they have planned anything for the next day. It seems like a refrain to the general tune of human life.

One reason why we now locate the Golden Age in the future is that we *know* it was not in the past. In a time of exact history we can no longer believe that the age of the Antonines, or any other past age, was more fortunate than ours.

Is the fall better or the spring? From the middle of February to June we live in hope and disappointment; the days grow brighter and longer, there are warm and prophetic hours, but the actual weather is, on the whole, the worst of the year. The autumn has a sad outlook from serene days. Are not most of us happier in the spring?

You tell me that the Greeks loved life for itself, while we follow illusions. But if I feel life as a growth, and so need to bring the future into the present, do I any the less love life for itself? To study humanity and plan a better future for it is no more an illusion than to plant tulip bulbs in the fall.

A WISE man will maintain a just relation between proximate and distant aims, keeping the former as definite and the latter as high as he can. It is enervating to dream of castles in Spain towards which you have no itinerary. It is not gloating misers who get rich beyond the dreams of avarice, but men who study the ways of trade and finance, nor are women won by mooning lovers, but by character and action. The sort of imagination that brings success is one that sees a distant summit, a general route to it, and just where to put your feet for the next ten steps.

WHAT we enjoy most is activity that is pleasant in itself and also hopeful for the future, as building a garage for one's car, preparing a garden, assorting notes for a book. There is a glamour on such things. What ends in the moment, like savory food, or games, or even beauty or passion, seems, when the mind rests upon it, to baulk our human nature a little. We need to live *for* something, to discipline and enhance the present by a larger aim.

WE ought to distinguish between a real future or rational extension of the present, consisting of the logical and not too remote development of actual conditions, and one which is unreal. To plan for the former is a reasonable function of the mind and every man's duty. The latter is beyond our scope, we have no business with it. If we permit ourselves to form conceptions of general purpose and destiny in life let us be aware that these are only symbols for our faith and loyalty. To fail to make this distinction, to demand to know what life is for and what the world is coming to, agitating in a vacuum those powers whose only use is to deal with facts, is merely a sort of running loose, like an engine without a load.

The End of the World

THE apprehension of general calamity, the horror, for example, that we feel at the thought of the extinction of mankind by the chilling of the earth, or collision with another planet, has little to do with time. It is not a real future because, although it may be logical enough on the astronomic side, a reasonable part of that system, we have no power to project our human system beyond, say, a century or two. It is just a bad dream. Whether we think of it as occurring ten years hence or a billion makes no difference, to think of it at all shatters our sense of security. Time does not enter. Time exists for us only in so far as we perceive a sequence of events to mark it by.

The Transitive Attitude

THE transitive man is one whose need is to pass over into achievement, to do things, and hence to have before him a vista of things worth doing. He sees the present as the open door to an efficacious future. Not always a rosy optimist, he is perhaps aware that disappointment may await him, but he does not dwell upon that, taking life in the onward sense to which his active impulses incline him. He is usually somewhat self-absorbed, an egotist if you please, but apt to give himself to large causes because they offer the amplest scope to the imagination. He may seem something of a mystic; there is perhaps an inward smile, when he speaks of his cause, that sometimes lingers in a habitual radiance like that of lovers. Or he may take on in conflict a stern and combative front. In any case he is more or less of an apostle, a propagandist, an incarnation of the hypothesis that the onward process of life is worth while.

THE transitive attitude was always natural to strenuous minds, but it seems somewhat special to our time, being fostered by the habit of striving, the growth of power and knowledge, in which we live. American life organizes it in innumerable forward looking associations and in a popular literature of hope and incitement. Teamwork is involved in it, and the habit of judging persons by their contribution to a common ideal. It runs through our whole psychology, children are brought up in it, and we require of life at large that it be constructive and hopeful. God himself must not be idle but appear to us in the process of creation.

TRANSITIVE minds are formed by their ideal, and will find beauty and repose only when that ideal is a work of serene art.

For an active spirit a high and remote aim is a great part of religion. It provides an object of faith and contemplation, raised above the fluctuations of the time, on which the mind may securely rest. Failure and uncertainty attend your immediate endeavors, but the distant hope remains, a light by which to compose and organize your thoughts.

IT seems that in affairs the whole conception of merit is becoming transitive. That is, the "good man" is not one who fits permanently into a function but one who is moving through and beyond it. Thus he will do his present work the better, it is thought, because he sees it in perspective, and will also diffuse an onward and creative spirit.

There is much in this, but I like also those who renounce ambition and cultivate gardens.

Posthumous Fame

WE have been discussing why men desire to be famous after death. I take it that what we really desire is to be enabled to think of ourselves as occupying an assured and honorable place in the minds of men. Time has little to do with it, except that if we have no such place now, and no immediate prospect of it, we have to assign it to the somewhat remote future. The main thing is to have the idea of it *now.*

The desire for future glory is also a matter of fashion, prevailing much more at some periods than at others, and we entertain it from emulation, which always makes us want to gain, and to have the credit of gaining, what others are striving for.

And so with the desire to be remembered and loved by our friends. Wherever and whenever they may be we need to think that a warm thought of us abides in them. Desire follows imagination without regard to time.

Might and Right

THE will to power springs from the active instincts of human nature; the will to righteousness from the need, also instinctive, to mould action into a consistent whole. Neither is more original or causative than the other: Might goes to make Right and Right to make Might; life is a progressive adjustment between them.

Prudence

PRUDENCE and compromise are necessary means, but every man should have an imprudent end which he will not compromise.

IT is better to conform in things you deem unimportant, but importance may be symbolic. To declare your general intention of dissent, by some outward form like the Salvation Army uniform, may be worth while as making all non-conformity easier. It is then expected of you.

That conspicuously disreputable garb with which R. L. Stevenson flouted Edinburgh, was it not the symbol and corroboration *to himself* of an escape from convention which he needed and was determined to have?

To turn the other cheek, whether right or not, is impossible for most of us without loss of self-respect, because we do not continuously *feel* that it is right. It is better in practice to remember that when one has treated you offensively you can almost always, if you control your resentment, think of a way by which you may assert yourself, gain a moral advantage over him, if you care for it, and yet not make an enemy.

When and how a man should assert his pecuniary right is largely a matter of the economy of energy. A student, since he needs quiet, should commonly avoid agitation by seeking no more than is clearly his due, and take dispassionate advice as to that. But he must have resolution to fight if driven to it. Cowardice is shameful here as elsewhere, and brings no peace of mind.

Peace of mind depends upon knowing that you can trust yourself to do the right and brave thing at the critical moment; and this comes from the habit of so doing.

Mark the tender spots of your opponent, but do not hit him on them if you can avoid it. Malice makes an enemy.

We may judge a man's ability by three things: by what he has done (including the impression he has made on others), by what he himself appears to believe he can do, by our own dramatic imagination, based on his immediate personality, of what he might do. If these do not agree it is prudent to observe him further.

Nothing is more a matter of habit than executive ability and immediate power over men. They require natural energy, insight and clarity of mind, but the transformation of these into address, equanimity, large vision of affairs and the air of authority, comes by practice.

Most of us avoid association with the unsuccessful. It is partly that they make us vaguely uncomfortable—as if we ought to do something about it—and partly from a feeling that failure may be contagious, or because we do not like to be seen in connection with it.

There is something not unlike this in the dogmatic optimism that refuses to see any painful side to life. It is drawing in our skirts and crossing to the other side.

FAILURE sometimes enlarges the spirit. You have to fall back upon humanity and God.

A TALENT somewhat above mediocrity, shrewd and not too sensitive, is more likely to rise in the world than genius, which is apt to be perturbable and to wear itself out before fruition.

BOYS are urged to hard work. This, for most, is needed advice, but there are very ardent spirits to whom some one should say, "Do not strain yourself. Quantity counts little without quality, which is raised by working moderately, though steadily, and by much thinking and planning. Conduct your life intelligently and you will be effectual without exhausting effort."

MOST of us live in cages whose bars are our own habits and fears. To break out, to get the habit of breaking out, is a prime need, and a few days or weeks of brave idleness are sometimes of more value than a year of work.

THE current wisdom is devised for the prevailing types of mind and body and to support the prevailing institutions. Divergent individuals must work out their own rules—often just the opposite. And even for the prevailing types most precepts prove transitory. How many rules of health, believed indispensable in their day, urged upon all of us as a duty and imposed by missionaries upon the heathen, have I seen discredited and abandoned!

PEOPLE *talk* most about things, but what they *feel* most is spirit, personality. That does the real work, even the rough work. We invent tangible reasons for beliefs and acts that are really due to the intangible. Personal impressions hover over affairs like invisible daimons, working strange victories and defeats.

Worry

WORRY is a tremulous agitation of the will, destroying peace and sleep. It seems to spring from a poor tone of the mind, (due to strain or ill health), and a troubling thought. Another source is a too strenuous habit of decision that some of us have, so that we cannot bear to leave a matter in doubt, though we are in no case to settle it. Worry is a frequent cause of failure: success requires a certain unexcited continuity of endeavor. An anxious man is soon tired, and, knowing this, is apt to lack courage. Others see his weakness and take advantage of it.

"Lighten mine eyes. . . .

Lest mine enemy say, 'I have prevailed against him'; And those that trouble me rejoice when I am moved."*

SMALL worries are worst when we are idle and are often dispersed by motion like a flock of gnats.

THERE is a discipline for ideas as well as for persons, and every thought is harmful that is not kept in order by a larger thought.

WHEN one first becomes aware of a disturbing event his mind has all it can do to effect the unconscious adjustments, to heal the first pains; it is not yet the time for thinking. Let the matter lie and it may work itself to a conclusion. At least it will mature until the ripe decision may be plucked by a little effort. People who dislike doubt often get into worse trouble by committing themselves to an immature and untenable decision.

There are two conditions of success difficult to combine: one the power to think clearly and decisively at the right time, the other the power to leave things undecided, without worry, at other times.

Distraction

IT is a chief use of social institutions to make up our minds for us, and when, in times of confusion, they fail to do this, there is more mind-work than most of us are equal to.

SOME think there can be no peace of mind in the complexity of modern life; but if we gain some understanding of this complexity, or at least a settled way of thinking about it, will it not seem reasonable and the ordered work of God?

THOSE conflicts with other persons which so distract and exhaust us are usually in the mind only and are in fact conflicts between the imagined thoughts and feelings of the other person, and our own, with all the emotional disturbance, the angers, fears, doubts and self-justifying dialogues thus aroused. If we shut out the other's view there is no conflict, and we can proceed on our ruthless way in peace. This men of affairs

* Psalm XIII.

mostly do. But if we admit the opposing idea the only way to abate the conflict is to work out a just view and follow it. If we can become so impenetrably sure we are right that the question ceases to exist for us, there is again no conflict. But who can do this?

THERE is no suffering like that of mental disintegration, the rending of uncontrollable impulses. Anything can be borne by the mind that is not felt to be destructive of the mind itself, but I doubt whether any one can say, "Thy Will be done," when he feels his very soul going to pieces. This is the supreme hazard of life. To lose sanity is to lose God.

But for one case of real danger there are a thousand that are imaginary. One finds himself, at intervals, in distractions which seem capable of breaking down his health or even his reason. In fact these troubles prove transitory and are, in the retrospect, unimportant.

Mental Management

I CAN have that opinion about anything which I ought to have," says Marcus Aurelius. If it were true that the will has unlimited power over the mind we should have nothing to fear; we could adapt our thoughts to the situation and nothing could harm us. But it is far from true: life can and often does impair the mind in spite of the efforts of the will to meet it. We should strive for adaptation but that we can always win is a false, though sometimes a useful, dogma.

OLD thoughts newly conceived give a fresh impulse. I resort now and then to that book of Epictetus (John Evelyn always carried it in his pocket and calls it an "incomparable guard") in which he reiterates the distinction between things in our power—our mental life—and things not in our power—behavior of others, reputation, possessions—exhorting us to fix our aims on the former and be chipping off new accretions of the latter. To control our own attitude is indeed an enterprise in which we may always look for some success. No doubt, however, this skill to untangle ourselves from the world of things not in our power may be too much cultivated. We are tied together for the common good, like Alpine climbers, and must not seek a private safety by cutting the rope.

IT is the ambition to seem that is distracting. The ambition to become, finding gradual but secure realization, brings neither despair nor elation.

LARGE contemplative truths never keep one awake nights nor make his heart beat too fast.

IT is no small part of the tactics of life to form the habit of making decision when your spirit is fresh, as in the forenoon, and ignoring midnight apprehensions. To let dark moods lead is like choosing cowards to command armies.

AS soon as one thinks to take life easier and store up energy for calmer and better work, the vital force streams out of cracks near the top of the filling vessel, and he saves only to waste. He grows sensual, gloating, captious, erratic. Only a somewhat severe application keeps one to his right self.

FROM time to time mind-cure fads appear and flourish. I have had help from them, and from auto-suggestive formulas of my own device. You can often save energy in this way and gain a healthy attitude towards trouble and disease. The new doctrines are essentially like the old ones, but novelty and the contagion of the crowd give any idea fresh power to take hold of us.

It is a way of building the will. To will anything you must have a thought-pattern to follow, and to form one is the hardest part of the process. By the aid of a teacher or a printed manual you are led to do this, and having the pattern before you it is easy to release energy into the prepared channel. But there must be energy; when there is a real and not a merely apparent depletion of force all methods fail, and auto-suggestionists yield in time to wounds, germs or age like the rest of us.

I soon tire of any mechanism, and find that the great books of the inner life—as Marcus Aurelius, Thomas a Kempis, Pascal, Thoreau and Emerson—last better than manuals. Being persons not schemes, they are not easily exhausted.

IT is my experience that no method whatever will surely drive off an obsessing idea, as of resentment, fear, suspicion or distracting uncertainty; but that if one can adopt a resolute attitude towards it, and go on living an ordered life in spite of it, it will presently wear itself out and pass away.

THE ascetic is an artist; he selects and controls his human nature in order that it may be, according to a certain plan, harmonious and beautiful. It is only in the extreme that his becomes a narrow and futile art, a mere refuge for timid spirits.

SENSUALITY is controlled by convention; we do not let others see us doing what is held to be shameful. As to what is not definitely condemned, or may be done in secret, I take it that life is an unremitting conflict, more or less strenuous according to temperament and conditions, between impulse and conscience. It is more strenuous the more we expect of ourselves; hence in youth and with ardent spirits; the older or more phlegmatic find a rut. In general, if one does not in any way cultivate sensuality, if his trend is above and away from it, so that it prevails only in occasional outbreaks, he may hope to gain upon and overcome it.

IN spite of iconoclastic moralists it remains true that the distinction of the human mind, as compared with the animal, is discipline, organization, the rational control of impulse. We have become what we are by that in us which makes us renounce the nearer and lower good for the higher and more remote.

CONSCIENCE is much depreciated by younger moralists who often assume it to be the voice of the past. More truly it may be described as a continuing drama in the mind, a running fight between an ideal and whatever clashes with it. All depends, then, on the ideal, which may well look not to the past but to the future.

Compensation

THERE is no mathematical law of compensation, as you might think from Emerson's essay on the subject. Now it more than makes up for the evil, again there is no compensation at all. Much depends upon your attitude, as confident or otherwise, and upon what energy you have to assimilate or transform the hurt.

IF the student were not restless he would never achieve anything; if it were easy for him to deal with the world he would not cherish recondite ambitions; if he loved men more he would love truth less.

DAYS of sickness and languor interrupt routine and often bring large releasing thoughts. One is abnormally sensitive to impressions of beauty and has sometimes a more visual perception of ideas.

THERE is a comfortable degree of deafness which is not without benefit to a scholar. It brings exemption from small noises by day and night; an excuse for avoiding parties, meetings, lectures and concerts; and, generally, the ability to ignore without offence utterances to which You do not care to listen.

WITH all our virtuous efforts to help our associates we often serve them best by those deficiencies for which they have to compensate.

THE Grace of God! I do not wonder that Christians have thought in this way of certain unlooked-for motions of the spirit, clear bright and warm as the sun breaking from clouds after a storm.

"How fresh, O Lord, how sweet and clean
Are thy returns, e'en as the flowers in spring;
Who would have thought my shrivel'd heart
Could have recovered greenness?"*

* George Herbert, The Flower

Part Seven

Larger Life

Faith

FAITH is a settled way of thinking favorable to endeavor and hope. We need it in action as a motive, in rest as a bar to doubt and fear. Human nature will make a faith, or accept one ready-made, unless the confusion of experience, reflected in a confusion of ideas, makes this impossible.

What sort of a settled way of thinking is possible depends upon the material that life pours in upon us. It cannot be the same for two epochs, hardly for two individuals.

I DOUBT whether any specific conviction about life is essential to faith. It is not indispensable that we should look upon it as good, in any usual sense, much less need we believe in a life after death. Probably any conception of the world as a place or order, as the expression of a power not anarchic, is reconcilable with faith. A man can be content to live and strive without the promise either of happiness or immortality, if only he feels that something worthy, some part of a great whole, is being accomplished in him. He is willing to be a humble soldier if he has confidence in his general; not a confidence that his general means to do something *for him,* but that he means greatly, in his own way.

IN what sense is faith an impulse of human nature? In the sense that we need to respect our own endeavors, and hence to believe in something that will give reality and meaning to them. The soldier must believe in his country; and if the workman cannot believe in his work, his employer or the industrial system, he may in Socialism or the Union. A woman needs to believe in her son, in her husband if she really accepts him. An author unwelcomed by his contemporaries has faith that posterity will cherish his works.

Faith and effectiveness support each other. Effective men make a faith for themselves because their active powers need it to rest on, and men of faith are effective, because of their courage and constancy.

As to what is beyond knowledge it is natural to believe what we need to be true, what helps us to live. By thus believing we help the world along, and if the letter of our belief turns out to be mistaken yet the spirit has served. We should remember that all such beliefs are provisional and not be too much put out when we have to give them up. Indeed we practice this; we believe in a thousand things long enough to try them out, and abandon or modify them accordingly.

One feels in himself the impulse of creation; if he can see in the world a like impulse, already organized and working, he can merge himself in that and be at peace. "My Father worketh even until now, and I work."

There is often a kind of faith, you might say a kind of piety, in the man of affairs. He believes in life; he believes that things are worth doing, that it pays to do them well, that nothing happens without a cause. To believe even in "business principles" is something.

Faith in our associates is part of our faith in God.

The faith state often implies a closing of the mind to unsettling problems. You may have a sense of unity with the Infinite if you exclude doubt, but on the intellectual battle front there will be conflict and uncertainty, and if minds are wounded it may be because they prefer to charge the enemy rather than stay in the trenches. The "surrender to Christ," after the way of the church, will give peace, joy, a new sense of life. So will a surrender to patriotism in war, or to any simple uplifting idea. The trouble is that many of us are in such a complex state that we cannot be simplified without being untrue to ourselves. It is too short a cut to blessedness. "Everything is all right" is a cheerful frame of mind, but is it moral? Are not the saints sometimes disgusting because of that self-satisfaction which they think of as peace with God?

As I grow older I feel more and more the need of faith in a larger process upon and in which my own activity floats, and which will go on whether I share it or not. A vague sense of the whole grows upon me, intangible, not to be scrutinized, yet supporting. In so far as I am aware of this whole I have assurance and joy, am calm and young. One passes out of the harassing passions of the smaller self onto the repose of a broad stream.

The Mind of the Soldier

MAN has what is in effect an instinct of devotion, whatever may be the psychology of it. He seeks a larger self to throw himself into—a cause, a country, a religion, an art, anything that will make great claims and open a new life. It is the appeal to this, sanctioned by collective emotion, that upsets our minds at the outbreak of a war.

THE hero of the War is human nature. The men of all the armies are deliberately meeting death rather than fail in duty. By thousands, by hundred thousands, they do it: they can no other: such, it appears, is man.

They seem not to question that they must be ready to die if honor requires it; the faith was already there. It makes theology look trivial.

I HAVE had many descriptions by intelligent young men of their state of mind on the field of battle. Few attribute much to patriotism, though it was no doubt in the background. The more immediate motives were a sense of honor and self-respect, such as impels one to do his duty anywhere. One of the best accounts summed them up as "bravery, conformity and adventure"; bravery meaning "the force that made them afraid to be unbrave," otherwise the need of honorable repute. Conformity would include congregate devotion; "We felt the sublime sentiment of every man who submerges himself in a common cause."

They are as unconscious of heroism as the criminal is of crime. These are attributions of society.

THE life of the soldier is for the most part passive, irresponsible, and this is one of the attractions of the service. "We liked the freedom of having a dead mind." Regular soldiers speak of their relief in joining the army after civil life.

The notion that war gratifies an "instinct of pugnacity" more than every-day conflicts is shallow. We do not need a moral equivalent for it in that sense. What we need a substitute for is its power to arouse congregate emotion and will.

EVERY system is more or less brutal to those whose minds do not fit into it. With a military system, such as America organized for the great war, the brutality is intensified by the purpose of the activity and by hurried and coercive methods. The whole thing was in many respects revolting, degrading; but what can you expect?

Such "bolshevism" as I have seen among American youth was learned in the American army.

The Lot of the Individual

THE individual human life, as we are now coming to see it, appears in no way isolated from life at large or alien to the general scene of nature. The creative energy everywhere at work, the Primal Love if you please, seems to have wrought out through the ages a continuing organism of itself, propagated in innumerable pulses of struggle, procreation and death. These pulses, as they rise and sink, are ourselves—passionate, venturing, tragic flashes of God.

NOT a few great names only, but all of us, suffer for a cause that grows by our decay. We need only to believe, like the dying soldier, that the cause and the leader are worthy, that we have fought a good fight. Indeed that we should believe this to the end is not necessary, only that it should sustain our active years. Faith is to work by. Our vision of the great life is perhaps only transient; ennui, chagrin, disappointment, and finally gathering insensibility and oblivion are in our lot. I expect that all that is merely mine, perhaps even faith, will fail.

SUMNER relates that an old chief of the Poncas, whose strength failed him as his tribe were migrating, asked to be left to die. "My children," said he, "our nation is poor, and it is necessary that you should all go to the country where you can get meat. My eyes are dimmed and my strength is no more. I am a burden to my children. I cannot go. Keep your hearts stout and think not of me. I am no longer good for anything."*

IT is not rare for the individual to think little of his own life in comparison with that of the group. It is probably the usual state of mind among savages, and among peasants, where there is an intense communal spirit. "The peasant does not greatly fear death for himself, but is terrified by a pest or war where the existence of his group is threatened."† The group he sees as the supreme and enduring form of life.

Is it not indeed the normal way of human life, of the mass of men in all ages, to live for a group, a heritage, a service, for some larger human whole, rather than for those aims that perish with the individual?

THE value of individual lives in general, or of the life of any particular individual, even in his own eyes, is mainly a matter of group opinion.

* W. G. Sumner, Folkways, 324.

† Park and Miller, Old World Traits Transplanted, 303.

THE joy of hopeful activity is enough to justify life. When I imagine myself dead and forgotten I feel no despair. I think of *our* life going on, and that seems enough. I could ill bear the thought of my work perishing, but I could dispense with any hope I may have that my name will be attached to it. I mean, not that I would willingly give up such a hope, but that its loss would not, so far as I can judge, seriously impair my exertions. I need to feel that I function in a human whole to the degree of my capacity, that I do not live in vain. But the acknowledgment of this function, through a name or a visual image, though stimulating, is not indispensable.

IT is grateful to think how well the world could do without me. I may, then, enjoy the spectacle.

THE current of life flows on bearing some of us on the surface in sunlight and joy; others, or ourselves at another time, are rolled beneath the waters in darkness and suffocation. Sooner or later we all sink, but the stream flows still in splendor and beauty. We try to live on the top, to share the wide life, to help others up.

As to the Shortness of Life

PERHAPS we should not say that life is short. The only life we know has endured, as to its main stems, for unimaginable ages, and has no visible term. Our "expectation," as a race, is practically infinite, that is, it goes far beyond any plans we can make for it, any definite interest it can have for us.

THE ancient and Christian philosophers were preoccupied with the thought of death and of how to reconcile oneself to it. We, having a larger human outlook, and notwithstanding our doubts about Providence and a second life, have perhaps less need of such precepts. We see grandeur and hope in the life we have. Perhaps, indeed, these preoccupations are somewhat peculiar to certain systems of thought and not so universal as we have supposed.

GRANDMOTHER, about 80, is visiting in the east and sends home things she has bought for her house. "I don't suppose I shall live forever," she says, "but while I do live I don't see why I shouldn't live as if I expected to."

MAN lives both in that which is sensuously present—the sunshine, the walk, the bath, the food—and in his plans and ideals. So also he lives both in activities that have little common meaning—chiefly these same sensuous affairs—and in the social imaginations and strivings that are even more himself. His life is sensuous and ideal, private and social, transitory and immortal. When he needs a larger world it begins to appear, because those powers that create the need can also satisfy it. Sensuous man does not need a future, imaginative man can make one. Without imagination there is no fear of death, with it we may live above that fear in a greater life.

It is not unnatural that we should live in the view of continuing life. When man, becoming an imaginative and creative animal, began to hand on a social heritage, he at the same time transcended, in a manner, his individual mortality and came to dwell in a common and undying whole. Our minds are free to move in the general flow of higher life preserved to endure beyond the individual term, and when we live understandingly we are formed by a select heritage and derive from it our aims. There should require no especial effort, no peculiar virtue, to live for eternal things, we are by nature of them. How should I who read Marcus Aurelius and Dante and Goethe not live in the same life in which they lived? No doubt my consciousness is involved with a physical organism and will cease when that decays, but while it lasts it shares in a continuing whole, made of a million such, and contributes to the common growth. Why should I spend any part of this three or four score years of glorious participation in wishing for more years which apparently I cannot have and which I should hardly want if I could?

All truth is beautiful when it shines largely over life, and so it is with that of the inevitability of death.

Evolution

Those fossil creatures in the National Museum seem to say, "I am on the map too; I made good; you wouldn't think I could do it in this way, but I did." From the crudest fossil to the ideal men in the adjacent art galleries all hangs together, is clearly one life.

It has a calming and enlarging effect if one remembers that he and all men, along with the other animals, are the offshoots of a common life. How, thinking thus, can one look upon his fellows except as brothers, or how appropriate anything he does as separately his? If I do a good work it is the central power working through me. This, says Thomas à Kempis, is the truth, by which one escapes vainglory.

CAN an evolutionist be anything but a true believer? How much more satisfying to the intellect is the all-pervading life process being revealed to us than theological imaginations which can be nothing more than reflections of ourselves. This is a *real* God.

IS not Darwin the chief modern theologian, since he made the largest and most fruitful study of how God works?

Expansion

IT is good to feel oneself part of a great whole, to expand the individual life into that, to cherish that part of oneself that contributes to the whole, to estimate oneself and others by capacity to serve the whole. The more you can do this the less you will be troubled by doubt, apprehension or personal chagrin. You will not take personality too seriously.

WE are merging into larger and more organic wholes of thought and life. Our institutions no longer have the separateness they seemed to have, individuals appear aspects of a social order, mind and body are phases of a single process, the epochs of history draw together, past, present and future are but one.

Solidarity

THE actual interdependence of human life, of persons, classes, nations, far surpasses our awareness of it, and still more our arrangements for cooperation. Wisdom is largely the perception of this interdependence, and the endeavor to give it organs.

We are, in truth, one with the great life. Our success lies in being so, not stupidly or sulkily, like unruly children sent to school, but with intelligence and will.

RUSSIAN peasants are reported to build close together so that no one will dare to set his neighbor's house on fire, as, from petty quarrels, some of them would otherwise do. We all have this kind of solidarity, but it does not prevent our starting little blazes which we think will do no harm to ourselves.

AS we come to see how many sources there are for events we have less confidence in any one scheme of betterment, any one person, class, race or nation; but more in what all can do by team-work in a common spirit.

THE erratic or selfish impulses of men mostly counteract one another; their higher strivings are more nearly parallel, and join to make a great current. The world has always been full of conflict, hate, destruction; but beauty, love and power have grown in the midst of them.

WE accomplish little except as we get into a current which will bear us on without great effort. This may be a current prepared by institutions, or it may be one which we have created in our own character by sustained endeavor. The former is so necessary that in any period of confusion individual talents are largely ineffective.

A MIND working without fellowship does not get the ripeness and flavor of a group development. It can rarely carry through a great design in art or literature with that equanimity, that mellowing unconsciousness, that yields a perfect fruit.

IT seems that for a time the Greeks, or those of them who bore the higher culture, saw life whole, clearly, passionately, and had withal the perfected technique to express it. The great men wrought simply; Phidias was unintrospective, had "serene spontaneity of action." This can only be when a man is swimming with the current of his age. Otherwise one can be whole only by struggle, and then imperfectly.

A VINE may die to the ground but a new one will grow from the root far more vigorously than from a seed. And so old tendencies in literature and society may disappear, but a concealed potency remains to give life to new shoots of the same kind.

IT is the idea of science that each scholar is a disciplined yet indispensable member of an imperishable whole. Every human occupation should have a spirit like this. If it is worth doing at all it needs continuity, tradition, emulation, the sense of contributing to an undying life.

OUR institutions are, on the whole, more rational than most individuals are most of the time. They express the more constructive activities of the more constructive men. One who studies them with an open mind, and observes also what happens when institutions break down, must acknowledge their workability, their relative beneficence.

To visit the insane reveals the unity of human life, for if these are not the fringes of a whole what are they? They seem the ragged outskirts of mind, the slums of the city of God. Surely they are not independent individuals.

I heard an idiot boy laughing loudly at the continuous cursing of a demented old man, heard him and sympathized with him, felt the merriment in his laugh, entered into his soul so far.

Every person, in so far as I understand him, is a part of myself, a phase of that "we" which all express. Every face is a window of the general soul, through which we may see into some apartment of the building.

Perplexity

When we are perplexed we project the disorder of our minds in a belief that the world is anarchical.

There is much talk of the chaotic character of human life. It is, in fact, a tangled growth, but always sequent, always proceeding from roots, like the vines and brambles in the swamp. You may not be able to get through, you may be entangled, lost, destroyed, but the life itself is orderly—delicately, beautifully so, if you could stop to examine it.

One sees life only as he has the fulness of spirit to enter into it. In our time of overflowing power we see the order, the brightess and the many colors; but as we grow old our vision fails, perhaps, and we stumble on in a dark and treacherous world. It remains all we ever saw, and more, but our years of seeing are few.

Are not those who nurse their egos on contempt of humanity—"the herd in the slime" and that sort of thing—hurt spirits who compensate in this way for a sense of inequality to life? They may have remarkable powers, like Nietzsche, but are never robust and sane. They lack, especially, a sense of humor.

To disinterested observation human life is just nature, the latest thing in growth.

The Incredibility of Institutions

NOTHING but the daily sequence of events enables us to believe in our institutions. Why should distant men remit me money, or students assemble in my classroom? Think of almost anything that goes on and ask yourself whether it would have been credible if you had not seen it. I notice that when I am removed from usual conditions I begin to doubt their existence. No wonder that men thrown out of their rut lose their grip on life.

Past, Present and Future

MAN is formed to be member of a social whole embracing not only the men of his lifetime but those past and to come. To live in the present only is as unnatural as to live in solitude.

PAST, Present and Future are only aspects of our thought; there never actually is any past or future, only a voyaging present. They are look-outs, fore and aft, to help us guide the course of the vessel. And we often attend too anxiously to what they say, or climb into the crosstrees ourselves, forgetting that our first business is to stay on deck and work the ship.

THE present moment, like every particular phase of life, should be thought of both as an end in itself and as contributing to a larger whole. If you neglect either of these you impair both.

Ideas About God

THERE are, and perhaps always have been, men who see religion in a dry light and comprehend it better than any believers do, but since they are not in warm enough sympathy with the religious to feel what they require, the actual growth of belief and worship will take such by surprise.

RELIGION can hardly withstand science in the province of the knowable, and is likely more and more to avoid a conflict. But in the limitless regions of speculation and sentiment left open to them the religious inclinations will continue to expatiate and to build a world according to their needs.

SPECULATION about God is for the most part slightly morbid or merely curious; a clear flow of life and purpose is himself, and all we need.

ANY definite idea of God must be trivial or fatuous: there is no way to know him but by knowing life, and we do that by living as largely, faithfully and thoughtfully as we can.

THE actual God of many Americans, perhaps of most, is simply the current of American life, which is large and hopeful enough to employ all the idealism they have.

IT is possible to think of life merely in terms of more or less knowable details—star systems, electrons, races of plants and animals, germ-cells, people, societies. This is the scientific way. But if we yield to the craving to conceive it as a whole, we can most easily do so in vaguely personal terms. We must use such thought-patterns as we have, and of these personality, however inadequate, is not only the highest but the only high one that all men have in common.

WE do not have to choose between God as a mechanism and God as a person. More logical than either, perhaps, as an inference from life, is the idea of a creative growth, of which persons are but one manifestation.

IF science should bring about an intelligible fusion of conscious life with the physical processes of nature, so that we could see them as one, it would be easy to conceive God in a similar unity. As it is we approach him from distinct standpoints and arrive at incompatible results. The God of human love and the God of cosmic law do not easily mix.

IT signifies little, nowadays, when men say they do or do not believe in God. Some think they do because they have an external and inert idea of him, others think they do not because their idea is too real to have definable form.

BY continually recurring to any thought the mind gradually gives it a sensible body; it becomes more and more an image, seems more real and cogent. So any settled way of thinking about life tends to become, in effect, an idea of God.

OUR conceptions of the unknown are only tools, and we may give them any shape that will do the work. Any hope, any faith, that works in us for good is justified in essence, because it is reasonable to assume that God is all we can conceive and more. The difficulty is to decide which *do,* on the whole, work for good.

THERE may be somewhere an all-foreseeing consciousness, but what we know of life is not like the work of such a consciousness; it appears to be, rather, the mighty and impulsive growth of a power that *feels its way* into incarnation. God is apparently a process, an onward-striving life, and we are members of him, real agents in his work, our conscience is his command. No intelligence planned the slaughter and filth of the Great War. We win our battles as we can, and so, perhaps, must God.

WHEN I say there is a building spirit apparent in life, you demand to know just what it is building. That is precisely what we are privileged—little by little and through the most alluring studies—to discover.

IF we considered seriously any of the ideas of God that men have formed in the past, asking whether we should wish them to be true, we should answer, "No, that wouldn't do at all; things are far better as they are."

SPINOZA's impersonal idea of God is one suited to a contemplative intellect, loving unity of thought and not needing personal support. It is made on the plan of what he felt as the higher part of his own nature. The love of God, according to him, is nothing else than "the rational contemplation of the order of the world, and of human nature as part thereof." He sought peace and freedom from passion in determinism, "for the knowledge of a thing as determined by definite causes tends to prevent us from fixing any emotion upon it." In a mind as active as his such a belief would not lead to sluggishness. So all such ideas are relative to the time, the group, the temperament and even the mood of those who hold them.

FOR moral use God must be something more than the object of our wonder and contemplation; the God of Decision must be a strenuous God. The old theology had God and the Devil to be the two sides of this: we, thinking of life as a growth, must apparently think of an affirmative spirit struggling with inertia or perversion. God, then, is love, intelligence, righteousness, productivity, as against sensuality, ignorance, laxity and sloth.

God and Oneself

I NEED no proof of God beyond my own life. As I live he lives. The arguments are irrelevant.

To possess God is an achievement, the grasping and holding of a satisfying and unitary life. If we can live on that level we are saved.

So long as one can keep faith in God he will not lose self-respect; and those who respect themselves have always a sort of faith in God. Indeed the most unlovely kinds of self find a god to uphold them. Your god may be a real god for you, though to others he appear a devil.

Man is a coin with the self on one side and God on the other—in a very similar style of art.

La Rochefoucauld says that it is more shameful to distrust our friends than to be deceived by them. May we not apply this to God? "Though he slay me yet will I trust him." To impute magnanimity where there is none would be no ignoble error, and if indeed it has not appeared elsewhere in the universe let it begin with us.

I may call it conscience, I may call it the contending movements of life coming to decision in my brain, I may call it a deep self, I may call it the voice of God—all comes to much the same thing. It is authoritative, it is in a high sense necessary: I must listen and obey on pain of disintegration decay and despair.

Seeking God

Whatever leads one out into larger currents of life is an approach to God. In the growth of such approaches, chiefly, is to be found the religious progress of our time. In democracy (so far as we have it), in internationalism, in socialized education, in the social work movement, in every branch of science, we have an actual organization of the greater life.

All joyous, hopeful, upbuilding forms of life help us to believe in God—youth, love, art, the faith that lives in books. I suppose we are never so truly living in God as when we are working out our ideals, no matter what they are.

Our sense of a great life is hardly other than our sense of noble persons. To be loyal to them is to be loyal to God.

So far as I can be said to have any conception of God it is a composite, shifting thing, formed from many glimpses, most of which I have got from the words or gestures of men. It is truth, it is kindness, it is courage, it is patience, it comes in whatever is fresh and onward and faithful. It is never stronger upon me than when I think of the men of the past who strove and fell for the right as they saw it. I am ashamed to do less.

IT is well to feel that God is one common current in all men, and that he flows mainly in the involuntary processes. Thus the individual will is relieved of too great a burden; we know that our work counts, but only as a small part of a great whole. There is, after all, no danger that we shall by chance wander outside of God.

THE love of God, like the love of country, is so natural to man that it needs only congenial suggestions and institutions to become a habit. Like the other, also, it often exists without our being aware of it, until some crisis brings it out.

WE may believe what we will about the whole; but the visible part of it we must see precisely as it is. *That* we are meant to know. It is life; it is our only chance; we must make the most of it.

TO live in and for the great life is, I take it, the sum of the matter.

Another Life?

MAN is a noble animal, splendid in ashes and pompous in the grave." *
Because it is his abiding will to assert a boundless destiny.

THE proper field of *definite* hope is the life we know. That is the real future, the long rope we are spinning out of the short strands of personality. When it is healthily conceived man is content with a vague optimism regarding the unknown.

THE singers of Israel cared not for a private immortality or a mystic other world. The God their souls pant after is a participating God, a very present help in mortal trouble. The Psalms tell only of social yearnings and healthy, earthly hopes, hopes of rains and crops and children and a prosperous family line, of righteousness within the tribes, of wealth and power for the chosen nation and of destruction for the enemies of Zion.

IT is not enough that we should feel ourselves in a vast impersonal current of being; we need an individual hope, something we can work for, an enduring self. This, I think, is normally found in continuing social interests, but where these are inadequate it gives rise to the confident projection of a second life.

* Sir Thomas Browne, Urn Burial.

THE need of a personal immortality may come from egotism, as some assert, but it may come rather from a human warmth which must conceive the great life as an association of familiar persons. I cannot have you unless I am myself. It is like the need of a personal God.

If I were the kind of man that requires such beliefs I should no doubt strive to gain them, and let no theoretic doubts stand in the way. Whether men will continue to require them in such measure as to give them an organized prevalence I cannot tell: It may well be.

HAVING learned to see the person as inseparable from an organic social life I could not imagine him as living on unless that lived on also: if the individual soul abides society must abide too.

PEOPLE are interested and contented when they are occupied with some hopeful enterprise. This extends to enterprises which continue beyond individual life—as the building of families, churches, sciences, industries—so that if you can enlist men in causes, the problem of human contentment, even in the face of death, is mainly solved. The great thing, then, is to make life as a whole a cooperative and intelligible struggle in which we may merge our individualities and find an enduring hope.

Varieties of Idealism

THE spirit of man varies from age to age, but much less than its modes of utterance would lead us to think. The Greek mind saw the higher life as self-reliance and self-proportionment, the Christian as love and devotion to God. But God, as Christians conceive him, is a kind of self, and trust in him is self-reliance. The Greek like the Christian would die for his ideals, and perhaps in a similar spirit.

IF you specialize on a phase of right, as purity, withdrawing from the main current of life, you are more apt to realize it, but your withdrawal implies that the common man cannot be pure; by your extreme you justify the other extreme of the world.

In the time of St. Francis the idea of purity and peace through renunciation took form in a monastic brotherhood which was thought of as a repository for a goodness unsuitable to ordinary men. In our day we see that good and ill are aspects of a whole and do not attempt disjunction. We aim at marriage with less sensuality, money-earning with less greed, and self-assertion with less selfishness. We hope to better the whole as a whole.

ROMAN philosophers were much like early Christians in having small hope for the mass of the people or for social institutions. They were an elect group saving their own souls by pious exercises.

THE social idealism of the ancients is pathetic; it was a glimpse of things to which there was no road, which could not be approached except after disaster, oblivion and a new birth. We have, what they had not, a hopeful plan and method. There is no *impasse,* but an open way for large endeavors.

Can Christianity Survive?

THERE are those who expect that a universal religion will supplant Christianity, Islam and the rest, and a world commonwealth do away with the existing nations. I think not. I expect coöperation, but think it more likely to come about by the persistence of actual institutions and the gradual harmonization of their ideals. The unity of mankind will be no uniformity.

IN what sense, if any, can Christianity become a general principle of conduct? Certainly not as non-resistance and the foregoing of ambition; Thomas à Kempis and St. Francis are hardly the men to make the world move; theirs is only one kind of goodness.

It seems that the essential thing is a spirit of understanding other persons, and of the love and patience and justice that flow from this. This spirit is adaptable, entering into men according to their temperaments and circumstances, not at all Utopian but an incentive for every day.

JESUS lived the life of the common people, sharing and glorifying their hardships. Thus he stands for that spirit of brotherhood and mutual service which their life teaches them to value. He is a symbol of the wish to make over the world in such fashion as common people would have it.

The sentiments that he taught and illustrated are the strong sentiments—the lasting, the social, the fit, the evolutionary, if you will. They have the power of conscience and cooperative society as against the power of lower impulse: the onward life is theirs.

THE charge that Christianity inculcates a "slave morality" of submission might well be thought ironical in view of the pugnacity of historical Christians. Indeed a doctrine that teaches men to control their merely personal passions may well make them more willing and formidable contestants for causes. The Christian, having submitted to God, is in the right frame of mind to fight the enemies of God, whom he identifies with his own. If Christians are inert it is not due to their Christianity, but to ignorance, credulity, sloth and other vices common to mankind.

"BLESSED are the meek, for they shall inherit the earth." People scoff at this; but if it means, as it apparently does, that those peoples shall thrive that are subject to discipline, or meek before the Lord, it is good sense. Compare the 25th and 37th Psalms.

ALTHOUGH Christianity was never so pressed upon me as to disgust me (as has been the case with many), I have had more spiritual incitement from other books than from the New Testament.

THE great things of Christianity are the genius of its hero and its social organization, which, with all its sins, has been more effective in creating a heritage of workable faith than anything else we have.

THE example of Christ has the disadvantage that it is far from us in time, race, social state; it cannot take the place of contemporary incitement. But it may be superior to the latter as a symbol for this very reason: it is more generalized, typical and established in the common thought, has become a language charged with the aspiration of ages.

IT would be folly to discard the Christian tradition. To what else can we so effectively appeal on behalf of good understanding among classes, races and nations? At the least it includes a current of idealism capable of taking any channel into which we may lead it; whoever works in any humane cause will feel it bearing him up. Its failures are such as inhere in all institutions.

THE hope of Christianity lies in regaining its appeal to idealizing young men and women. It is formidable, this ardent youth that broods over the vision of Jesus, its own bright leader and sacrifice. It will easily brush aside ten times its number of hesitant sceptics: all it needs is a plan.

The Golden Rule

THE Golden Rule is a cherub with wings but no hands or feet. It is curious that there should have been so little thought and written by the great minds of the Church about its application to the intricacies of life.

It is an appeal to the imagination. It means, if it means anything, that we are to think and feel ourselves into the other man's place, see what he needs to have done, and then come back to our own place and do it.

THERE is no benefit without continuity—you might as well cut off a man's legs as his habits—and hence the first condition of well-doing anywhere in the human world is to understand what is already going on.

A RESOLUTE Christianity, which strives to act upon the Golden Rule, expecting others to do the same but not shaken when they do not, unflagging in consideration, capable of conflict but resourceful in avoiding it, is indeed as good a way of dealing with the world as one can hope to find.

THE Golden Rule is not acted upon because it demands knowledge and imagination, which are costly. It even demands social psychology. Think of the honest Christians in the Great War, ardently oblivious of the points of view of other nations. Think of them now, similarly oblivious of other classes and sects. Men will do almost anything rather than enlarge their minds.

There is a fine field for a real Christian science in the investigation and obviation of those ignorances, prejudices and illusions, those prepossessions of class, race sect, locality and nation, that keep the Golden Rule from being even faintly operative in the wider relations of life.

CAN we do anything more unchristian than to impair understanding—as when employers refuse to meet workmen, the press colors the news, censors and zealots of all sorts try to control teaching or discussion? It is a "sin against the Holy Ghost."

WE are impelled to understand others and do them a measure of justice not by our good will alone but also by their resistance, or that of some one else in their behalf, to our aggression. There is nothing more unchristian than mere non-resistance; it is salutary only when it includes a kind of spiritual attack.

OF 1000 nominal Christians 900 do not seriously wish to follow the Golden Rule. Ninety of the remaining hundred are blinded by class atmosphere to what it requires; and of the last ten, one, let us hope, intelligently carries it out.

Group Sins

A WRONG-DOING that is individual and conscious tears the spirit from that social tissue in which alone it can live. The wages of sin is death.

But who will convict us of our group sins? We practice these in a cheerful sense of fellowship, and with all the abandon of the social current. Conscience approves and our friends and leaders. Yet a glance at history shows them the most pernicious of all, engendering wars, oppressions and the virulence of sects and classes. This is the Devil whom we ignorantly worship.

CHRISTIAN devotion implies mental peace and a flow of love. But we get these mainly from the contagion of groups—of sects, nations, races, parties—whose activities as wholes are apt to be narrow, combative and anti-Christian. The individual specializes in love on condition that the group specializes in conflict. It would seem, then, that a total Christianity, not a part of life indulged at the expense of another part, awaits such a unification of ideal as shall reconcile group with group. But since conflict is of the essence of life I think that unification must include a measure of it, which, however, we may hope to render orderly, fruitful and not too unkindly.

Those very people who advocate mutual understanding, conference and the like, often deprecate such a spirit as enervating in time of struggle, not only in war but in civil conflict. It is felt, if not admitted, that there is a time for whole-hearted antagonism as well as one for consideration and compromise. One builds powers, the other tests them.

Social Religion

THERE is no religion for an active spirit that does not focus on a purpose capable of animating the highest powers he has. This must be social because his nature is so. It may be found in science or art, but for most of us it lies in some form of tangible and not too indirect service to that part of humanity with which we feel our unity.

It should, then, be the aim of religious leadership to clarify and illustrate our larger human purposes and bind them together into a whole.

THE best religious education would be one that accustomed us from childhood to cooperation—not too gregarious—in the service of human wholes. Through the family, the play-group, the school, the community, the nation, humanity, we might acquire an enlarging sense of God.

I CANNOT predict the forms which religious belief and worship will assume, but I think I can see that it will more and more idealize the solidarity of the individual with the race, and of all mankind in the ennobling of a common destiny.

Christianity and Class

THE situation of the rich in relation to the poor is essentially unchristian. It may be defensible, in economic theory, that one family should spend on itself five, ten, twenty, fifty, times the amount that (the total production being what it is) it is possible for the average family to have; but nothing will make this seem a kindly arrangement. A class of people thus privileged will of necessity feel towards the rest a mixture of pity and antagonism, the first for lacking what they themselves have come to think indispensable, and the second because of the underlying conflict of interests. They have the spoil and, however kindly disposed, are fighting to keep it. Unconsciously, perhaps, they cherish their own ignorance of the less privileged, and evolve or embrace theories of the incapacity or perversity of the poorer classes. What a relief to discover that the children you are crowding out of life are "the unfit"!

THE church may accept such conditions but the common-sense of mankind will not.

AFTER long study one comes back to the thought of childhood that no one ought to have more than is really necessary for his function, more than a wise Foreman over all the work would assign him.

The Church

CHRISTIANITY as the spirit of a teacher, and the Christian Church, are not only distinct but in great part contradictory. The church is an institution like others, and no more to be trusted—perhaps less, since the higher the ideal the more destructive of it is institutional mechanism. Yet it has had a great part in the past and may have a greater in the future. If it can cease to be a sect, broaden with the times and stand forth for the primary ideals of all men, it may yet function as the protagonist of the human conscience.

THOSE who are content with the church are just those who have not imagination enough to be Christians.

In the case of a priesthood a whole class of men are set up as the interpreters and examples of the highest life. Virtue is ascribed to them *ex officio,* and like the rest of us they accept that idea of themselves which they see in the minds of others. It is then inevitable that the coarser or weaker minded should assume sanctity; and so the common man, no longer in awe of the church, comes to think of the clergy, as a class, with disgust. He sees fatuous and sanctimonious faces.

With disgusting grossness the fine appeal of the young man of Nazareth has, through all the ages, been exploited by men of a wholly alien sort. Nothing breeds cynicism like the church. And yet through it the fine appeal does get dissemination.

The religious institutions of the future will be shaped by aggressive, socially-minded men, seeking a unitary conception of life and fellowship in humane striving. They will reject what is clearly at variance with fact, but in the sphere of speculation will accept any way of thinking that suits their working needs, possibly a very anthropomorphic God.

Salvation

THE quest of a great life, once organized in the old Christian Plan of Salvation, needs to be reorganized in social faith and education. Children may begin to find it in the school and community, as well as in the family. Opinion and cooperation may make it a habit of thought. If we think the whole we shall serve the whole. Let us "set the world in our hearts."

Too long we were taught that good will was the same as goodness. We now see that most evil is done by those who mean well. What we urgently want is knowledge—true perceptions of the working of each part on every other part in the common life of man.

The Christian emotion, that formerly had a somewhat technical character, owing to its exclusion from large fields of life, is coming more and more to embrace the community, the nation and the world in its range. It may lose some kinds of intensity, but gains in breadth, becoming more and more a kind of higher patriotism in which one feels oneself a member of a world-whole, and looks beyond that to God.

Democracy takes seriously the precept "unless ye become as little children." It seeks to make the world more and more such a one as the child asks for.

Index